Praise for unHeritage

This book, written by experienced wealth advisors, will guide your head, heart, and spirit to make legacy decisions that will inspire your family for generations to come.

Phil Cubeta
Wallace Chair in Philanthropy, American College of Financial Services

I highly recommend unHertitage to families (and their advisors) who want to pass on their values as well as their valuables.

Todd Fithian
Managing Partner, The Legacy Companies, LLC

There are few books that offer the opportunity for a "short read" while including ideas, information and opportunities to last a lifetime. This is one of those books; I highly recommend you make it a priority read.

Barbara A Culver
Founder, Connect-Gens, Cincinnati, Ohio

unHeritage is a must-read for successful families and their advisors. It covers the whole spectrum of areas needed to maintain a family heritage for future generations.

Johnne Syverson
President, Syverson Strege & Company (Past President of AiP)

unHeritage combines scriptural truths with practical wisdom to illuminate 11 pitfalls that can ensnare the most well-intentioned parents and grandparents. Your family will be the beneficiaries of the time and energy you devote to integrating unHeritage's best practices for family flourishing.

John "John A" Warnick
Attorney, Founder of the Purposeful Planning Institute

From the 11 pitfalls to the solutions and facilitation needed to avoid them, everyone interested in leaving a positive legacy will benefit from reading unHeritage.

Rod Zeeb, JD, HDP™
CEO, The Heritage Institute

unHeritage is definitely the lighthouse for protecting your family and wealth for generations. This book is a must read for anyone interested in legacy planning.

Enzo Calamo
Attorney and CEO, Lugen Family Office Inc.

Don't be fooled by the simplicity and readability of unHeritage. It identifies the key questions and provides straightforward answers that advisors and families alike should study and apply.

Scott Farnsworth, JD, CFP©
President, SunBridge, Inc., President, Main Street Philanthropy, Inc.

unHeritage provides a clear and concise roadmap for finishing well by choosing the positive alternative to the mistakes so many families wished their parents would have avoided.

David W. Holaday
Wealth Design Consultants, LLC

unHeritage will be tremendously helpful to our significant-net-worth client families. I plan on encouraging all of our clients to read it.

Scott Hamilton
CEO, InKnowVision, LLC

These authors write with great experience and wisdom. Because relational challenges can undermine even the best tax and financial planning, it is critically important to think deeply about the questions that unHeritage asks and answers.

Tim Voorhees, JD, MBA, AEP®
President, Voorhees Family Office Services, Inc.

Leaving a legacy is not an option; everyone leaves a legacy. One benefit of dealing with these 11 pitfalls earlier rather than later is the opportunity to live our legacy of choice today. I will share this book with many families from coast to coast.

Alan Pratt
President, Pratt Legacy Advisors

unHeritage

11 Pitfalls to Family Legacy
and How to Avoid Them

Contributing authors:
Tom Conway
Steve Gardner
Bill High
Jerry Nuerge
Ryan Zeeb

Editor:
Steve Gardner
Contributing editor:
Daryle Doden

familybrand
press

Published by Family Brand Press,
8301 Sagimore Court, Fort Wayne, IN 46835

www.centerforfamilyconversations.com

Unless otherwise noted, Scripture quotations are taken from

THE HOLY BIBLE, NEW INTERNATIONAL VERSION®, NIV® Copyright © 1973, 1978, 1984, 2011 by Biblica, Inc.® Used by permission. All rights reserved worldwide.

Other Scriptures are taken from the following:

New American Standard Bible®, Copyright © 1960, 1962, 1963, 1968, 1971, 1972, 1973, 1975, 1977, 1995 by The Lockman Foundation

Used by permission. (www.Lockman.org)

The Holy Bible, English Standard Version® (ESV®)
Copyright © 2001 by Crossway, a publishing ministry of Good News Publishers.
All rights reserved. ESV Text Edition: 2011

ISBN: 978-0-9916094-2-0

Library of Congress Control Number: 2014942767

Acknowledgements

The Center for Family Conversations gratefully acknowledges contributions to this project from many individuals and organizations.

Ambassador Enterprises
www.ambassador-enterprises.com

Camelot Portfolios
www.camelotportfolios.com

Kingdom Advisors
www.kingdomadvisors.org

National Christian Foundation
www.nationalchristian.com

Cover art was created by Indiana University-Purdue University Fort Wayne. Thank you, John Motz, Jamie Rinkenberger, and the rest of the class for your collaborative effort.

Interior page layout and art/imagery designed by Jamie Haughee.

Thank you, Gary Martin, for your management of vital processes in the development of CFC and this book.

Preface
DARYLE DODEN

From one elephant to another

Do you feel the target on your back? Do you sometimes sense that everyone wants a piece of you?

Speaking at a conference for nonprofit development people, I watched a presenter offer instructions on the care and feeding of elephants – mega donors. Much of what he said was accurate and helpful. But I couldn't shake the feeling that I was a marked man.

It's one thing to be sought because of who you are as a person – one who thinks and collaborates for noble purposes. It's quite another to be hunted because of what you have, your resources – your tusks.

With great privilege comes great responsibility. I get that. I want to meet my family's needs. I want to be a good steward – no, I want to be an excellent steward. And I want to enjoy God's blessing without irrational guilt. Most of us want that. The WHAT and WHY are the easy parts. It's the HOW that conceals all the snakes in the grass.

Sometimes I feel alone in this wilderness, wanting to be valued for who I am. Wanting to use my tusks to fulfill the purposes for which they were given me. Wanting to play the role for which God designed me.

This book has inspired and encouraged me. It has helped me realize that I'm not alone. There are others who have experienced my dilemma, whether as elephants or experienced advocates. I feel their presence on my side of the table, with my family's best interests at heart. They're helping me answer the HOW of putting my family in a position to thrive for generations, to avoid entitlement, and to become valuable contributors to their world.

Foreword
DAVID WILLS

Legacy.

It's not a long word. But it's a big word. In all the years I have served with the National Christian Foundation, I don't think I have ever heard a more joyful word and yet, at times, a more tragic word.

We've seen families who have done a remarkable job preparing their progeny to receive wealth. We've seen success into the second and third generations. What a joy it is to serve those families. They are models of health, serenity and discipline.

But we've also seen the other side – families who have been torn apart by wealth. We've seen the families with wayward children, non-communicative parents, and sibling rivalry.

Many factors contribute to the ills as well as the successes of families, but I think if I had to boil it down to one thing, I would say it comes down to a long view. This view involves how they see those that will come behind them and a truly eternal perspective on all that has been entrusted into their care.

*We need to return to a focus upon cultivation
of values for future generations.*

The wise farmer spends a great deal of time preparing and cultivating the soil before he plants. We've lost some of that – the long view – in our country. Too often we've become concerned about estate planning and taxes, and we've placed too much emphasis on the transfer of financial assets. We need to return to a focus upon cultivation of values for future generations.

In the pages that follow, you'll find some helpful insights from men I know and trust. They've done the hard work of helping families take the long view. It is not an exact science, but a sense of accumulated wisdom.

In this book you will see examples to follow, questions to ask, and counsel to consider. I pray that you'll read this book. React to it. Challenge your own thoughts. Consider deeply the truth that lies here. And then act upon it.

Our future generations depend on it.

For legacy,

David Wills
President, National Christian Foundation

Introduction

STEVE GARDNER

Regaining consciousness, 25-year-old Jackson Belmont IV strained under bright lights in a sterile room filled with machines, monitors, and tubes sticking into various parts of his body. "Where am I?" was his first question, followed quickly by "Why?"

Dr. Harundi aimed a light into Jackson's right eyeball and grunted. "You're in my ER again because of bad cocaine, just like the last time. The bigger 'why' is beyond me. You're the only one who can answer that."

It wasn't that Dr. Harundi didn't care. He had just seen too many Jackson Belmonts – kids of privilege throwing their lives away as if they had nothing to live for, nothing to contribute, no one to care about.

He had no way of knowing that the legendary Belmont fortune was all but gone and that Jackson's generation stood to inherit little beyond their well-developed sense of entitlement.

Money solves problems. Lots of money solves lots of problems. In the process, however, it inevitably creates some new problems – problems inadequately addressed by most estate planning. A long history of unintended consequences reveals the failure of estate planning to provide its intended benefits. Just ask Jackson's great grandfather.

Extreme makeover

Estate planning needs an extreme makeover. Growing recognition of this has led to a change in emphasis. Words like "heritage" and "legacy" have become commonplace in the wealth-transfer industry. Occasionally they signal a meaningful change in approach; sometimes they just amount to a new name on an old process.

Unfortunately, the old process, despite the best wills and trusts in the world, cannot survive eleven pitfalls.

Eleven pitfalls

1. Unidentified family values
2. Generational disconnect
3. Husband/wife disconnect
4. Lack of next-generation leadership
5. Wayward child
6. Indecision leads to inaction
7. Lack of a succession plan
8. Misunderstanding how to treat heirs – equally or uniquely
9. Lack of beneficial modeling
10. Lack of generosity
11. Undeveloped family story

There is a better way. Form should not dictate function. Accounting and legal procedures to preserve financial capital should not dictate the human outcomes you want to achieve. Good legacy planning puts the human outcomes first, because quality relationships – not quantity of dollars – ultimately define quality of life.

Good legacy planning requires good questions.

We learn from early childhood that choices have consequences and that we need to develop good judgment to weigh them appropriately. Whether consciously or subconsciously, we constantly ask ourselves questions; the quality of these questions often dictates the quality of the answers.

We begin with simple questions like "Is it safe?" and "Is it pleasurable?" As we mature emotionally – which is not as automatic as physical maturation – we transition to deeper questions:

1. What are the unintended consequences of taking the path of least resistance?
2. How likely are these consequences to occur?
3. On what am I relying to make me an exception to the rule?

4. What courses of action are available to me? What impact will one course of action have versus another?

5. What will the impact be on me, my family, my community?

The quality of our questions often dictates the quality of the answers.

Good legacy planning requires starting with the end in view.

As we develop the quality of our questions and thinking, we naturally develop another valuable strategy: starting with the end in view. Apply this to the heritage or legacy you are building. Why wait until you've reached the top of the ladder to realize that it's leaning against the wrong wall? Ask yourself: What are the highest aspirations I have for my children, grandchildren, and beyond? How will my money help or hinder these aspirations?

Good legacy planning puts the human outcomes first . . .

If Jackson's great grandparents had recognized the need to give more attention to preparing their heirs than preserving a fortune, the Belmont family story may have followed a different trajectory.

Good legacy planning requires learning from the experience of others.

One measure of our maturity is allowing the experience (and resulting wisdom) of others to play a stronger role in our deliberations. Why learn everything the hard way by assuming that we are somehow exempt from the consequences others have brought upon themselves? Why require our own personal pain to alert us to danger?

Great-grandpa Jack Belmont certainly hoped that Jackson IV, whom he could only imagine in the distant future, would experience a life of greater opportunity and value than his own.

He, like most wealth creators, spent more energy thinking about how he could create it than how he would distribute it, how it would produce the quality-of-life outcomes he wanted. Nothing wrong with his intentions – only with his inability to perceive the pitfalls ahead.

He would be shocked to see young Jackson in the ER. He would be angry over the squandering of the family fortune. And he would be crushed over the state of the family in general.

Although Jack may not have had access to the kind of help he needed, we can't make that claim today.

The authors of this book have helped others avoid the pitfalls to family legacy. Learn from them how to ask the right questions and start with the end in view.

Quality relationships – not quantity of dollars – ultimately define quality of life.

Quick Assess and Find Help

- Is lack of clarity causing you to postpone the process of legacy planning? See Chapter 6.

- Do you and your spouse have differing convictions regarding important elements such as asset distribution? See Chapter 3.

- Do you have a refined strategy for dealing fairly with heirs who vary greatly in interests, capacity, and responsibility? See Chapter 8.

- Are you clear on your role as a parent and confident in how you are performing it? See Chapter 9.

- Are you minimizing the risk of children rejecting your family's values? See Chapter 5.

- Do the various generations in your family fully accept, respect, and appreciate the others? See Chapter 2.

- Has your family identified and promoted its unique guiding principles? See Chapter 1.

- Is your family story (history of members and developmental highlights) recorded in a user-friendly format? See Chapter 11.

- Are you grooming young leaders within the family to assume strategic roles? See Chapter 4.

- Do you have a refined, actionable succession plan that will enable your business to thrive in your absence? See Chapter 7.

- Is your family working together in supporting worthy causes with time, talent, and treasure? See Chapter 10.

Pitfall 1

Unidentified family values

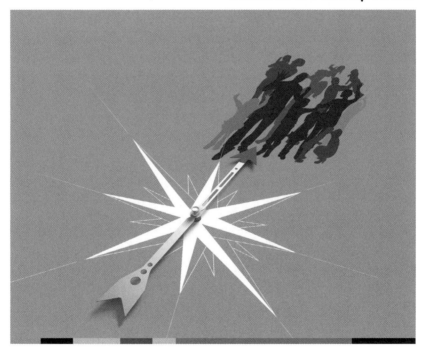

"Always make your future bigger than your past."

Dan Sullivan – Founder, The Strategic Coach

April 2014
(continued from the Introduction)

JB (Jackson Belmont III) excused himself from the country club's Spring Kickoff party and sped through light late-night traffic to the hospital where his son lay unconscious. *This kid's gonna be the death of me*, he thought.

Remembering his own college days forced him to acknowledge his own brand of foolishness. *But it's not the same*, he told himself. *I didn't keep pushing it to the edge of death. What is he thinking? Is he trying to prove something? Does he think he has nothing to live for? How have we gotten to this place?*

Chapter 1

The Family Compass
JERRY NUERGE

Modern life in developed economies presents a jungle of choices. Media bombards us with messages designed to create a sense of need combined with urgency. Knowing that consequences result from our choices, we feel pressure to make good decisions. The greater the consequences, the more angst we experience. As wealth increases, so do the stakes around its preservation and future use.

Corporations, faced with an endless array of opportunities and challenges, know the importance of carefully choosing their values and crafting a vision and mission to keep their energies focused. These provide a compass for navigating through their jungle of potential distractions.

Families often lack this compass for present and future decisions. Most high-net-worth people believe that if they have signed all the trust documents and wills, they have taken care of the future. After all, their attorneys and CPAs have assured them that the maximum amount of financial assets will be transferred to their spouse and then to their children with as little loss to the tax man as possible. Unfortunately, research shows that only ten percent of financial assets make it to the fourth generation.

Only ten percent of financial assets make it to the fourth generation. Ninety percent . . . gone . . . within four generations.

How can the results be so grim if the best attorneys and accountants money can buy are developing the estate plan? It is not because these folks are dishonest or uncaring. They have been trained to approach legacy strictly from the defensive perspective of tax planning and getting the greatest financial value to your loved ones. Some are absolute masters in accomplishing this goal, but it might not be the goal you desire – particularly if you think there are higher values than money.

I have been honored over the years to work with highly skilled attorneys and accountants on their own estate plans. In each case, they had produced very sound wills and trust arrangements for their heirs. But after answering a few questions and completing some exercises, they acknowledged that there were pieces missing from their plans – pieces they were not trained to assemble, but pieces that they acknowledged would multiply their family legacy by ten to twenty fold from where they were.

Although it has become fashionable for financial planners to call themselves legacy advisors, many of them add very little value to the old approach that has proven so inadequate. Raising your family legacy timeline from 25 or 30 years (one generation) to 100 plus years (fourth generation and beyond) requires a new kind of thinking and structuring.

A family's values are just as important as those of a corporation, but they receive far less attention. And even within corporations, the approach to them often yields little more than a filed document or perhaps a poster of high-sounding values that bear scant resemblance to daily business practices. I have found it much more beneficial to families to focus on three often-ignored components that have the potential to extend a legacy indefinitely. These are the family's values, virtues, and story.

1. What are our values?
2. What virtues will we pursue?
3. What do we want our family story to be?

Collectively, these are *family brand equity*, the core of a family's culture. The values define the family, the virtues build the family, and the story describes the family.

Values

The values discussion is an excellent entry point for collaborating on *family brand equity* matters. This kind of values discussion differs from exercises you've experienced in the past with other organizations. It is not intended to produce a list of noble sentiments – world peace, nature preservation, universal education – or high-sounding ideals – integrity, service, excellence. Rather, it captures the present reality of what family members value based on how they spend time and money. Health, security, entertainment, relationships, recreation, family gatherings, education, travel – these are just a sample of what might make your list. Think of what appeals to you without thoughts of what *should* appeal to you.

Discovering your honestly felt shared values is an important step in building transparency and unity within a family. When differing perspectives on other issues threaten the family's ability to function as a unit, appealing to deeply held shared values can soften divisions and frame the problem to be solved in a better light.

Without diminishing the importance of discovering our values as a family, we realize that it is not the answer to every long-term need a family faces. Even when coupled with the family story, there is still a missing piece. Human values fall short when it comes to making us moral. Clarifying values is a fine thing, but without an authoritative standard, values – like beauty – depend on the eye of the beholder.

So, rather than elevate whatever human values are currently in vogue in our culture, we identify our family's values based on the evidence of our calendar and pocketbook. Then we move to the second component of *family brand equity*, focusing on virtues that reflect God's character. These virtues foster strong relationships, creating a symbiotic community that can withstand the onslaught of individual failures to life's challenges.

Virtues

Virtues are frequently underestimated in importance. Aristotle argued that substantial happiness and human flourishing could be grasped only through the virtues. King Solomon stated it this way: "*My son, do not forget my teaching, but keep my commands in your heart, for they will prolong your life many years and bring you peace and prosperity. Let love and faithfulness never leave you*" (Proverbs 3:1-3).

Moral fiber within a family, like muscle within a body, naturally weakens with disuse. Weakened morality eventually incapacitates and destroys even the most powerful and wealthy of families.

The battle of morality is not so much about knowing what is right as it is doing what is right. Our conscience provides good guidance, but the gap between conscience and performance is what allows people to commit adultery when they know it is wrong. In such cases, value clarification is less important than virtue development.

People rationalize and modify their values based on conflicting desires. The result is immoral actions, which carry inevitable consequences. Virtues, on the other hand, are good, habitual actions of the will, revealed by the Designer and validated over time regardless of circumstances.

Virtues are part of a family's spiritual perspective or faith base that encourages each generation to live for more than self-service. Thinking more of others, ironically, leads to greater fulfillment. Acknowledging God's ultimate authority and trusting his guidance leads to a life of greater "peace and prosperity," as seen in Solomon's words.

Seven virtues

Seven common virtues span cultures, religions, and the test of time. Four of the seven – prudence (wisdom), justice (righteousness), fortitude (courage), and temperance (self-control) – are called cardinal virtues and are classified as moral virtues that can be acquired by human effort. It takes prudence to find our way, and justice to maintain a right standard. It takes fortitude to persevere in the face of conflict, and temperance to resist unhealthy indulgence.

Thinking more of others, ironically, leads to greater fulfillment.

The remaining three virtues – faith, hope, and charity – are classified as theological virtues that have God as their origin, motive, and object. They inform the moral virtues and give life to them.

Faith empowers us to believe in God and all that he has revealed. It is a striking paradox that faith has such solid assurance even though it focuses on something not yet visible, something real but unseen.

Our will, choosing to follow the direction of another authority, moves our intellect to accept something as true that it does not yet see to be true. The choice to accept something by faith begins by accepting that what we know by sight or current hard proof is limited. Faith surpasses rather than contradicts the limitations of our known reality.

Hope is desire coupled with faith. It looks to the future and empowers us to strive with confidence and expectation toward the achievement of something challenging – whether an accomplishment on earth or eternal presence with God. Hope begins with a base of faith and builds a bridge to the highest theological virtue, which is charity or love.

Love keeps our drive to achieve from becoming toxic.

Charity, in the broadest sense, is not just the act of giving; it is the act of loving. God, as the source of all virtues, commands us to love him above all else and to love our neighbor as ourselves. Love keeps our drive to achieve from becoming toxic.

Jesus described the greatest proof of love as being willing to lay down our life for a friend. When love rather than immediate self-interest motivates us, God rewards us with the ultimate self-interest of enduring joy.

Story

The family story is a crucial component. Having dealt with this in greater detail in Chapter 11, we'll summarize it as a written or digital document containing stories from each generation.

Think of the family story as an ongoing stream of past, present, and future stories of family members woven together. These stories, infused with the family's values and virtues, provide a deep sense of identity as well as motivation to not be the generation that weakens the heritage.

Value of *family brand equity*

Developing and communicating the *family brand equity* (values, virtues, and story) both verbally and by example preserve wealth. A growing body of evidence documents the importance of this compass in creating a heritage that strengthens and grows over multiple generations. The financial assets, instead of diminishing, increase because the value and virtue bases of the family increase.

Imagine the priceless joy when *family brand equity* is the focal point of our transfers to the next generation! These assets empower families to live intentionally productive lives for multiple generations.

Questions to avoid this pitfall

1. How do I determine the validity and accuracy of the compass by which our family currently navigates? What objective standards does it recognize?

2. What are we doing to encourage family members to share their individual stories with the family? Do we have a growing sense of how these individual stories blend to form our family story? How is it being honored and preserved?

3. What values currently drive time and money decisions of our family members? Which ones would be shared by most? How do I know?

4. How does our family pursue virtues and express its commitment to them?

Praise for unHeritage

I'm a bit of a book snob – so if a book doesn't "catch" me, I put it down. I read your book cover to cover! It is one of the most practical books on finances and legacy I have ever read. I can't wait to implement the steps you laid out in the book for my own succession plan. Thank you for writing such a timely book. No matter where you are in your career, you would benefit from reading unHeritage. Great Job!

John Faulkner
Founder & Editor in Chief, TwoTen Magazine

A massive body of statistics over the past half century shows that the viability of America's exceptional founding principles are most guaranteed by each new generation of children who start off their lives within permanent family and religious values and habits. CFC's family brand equity will have increasingly powerful benefits for all who have not had the advantage of family security and religious belief.

Dan Sullivan
Founder & President, The Strategic Coach, Inc.

They nailed it. The authors have isolated the deepest yearnings of wealthy Christians. Then they incisively condense decades of relevant experience into a few fast-paced pages. un-Heritage is deadly serious, quick to the point, and full of useable ideas and insights. It's rare to be able to say, "My life is different because of this book." This is such a book. It could change everything for you.

Patrick Morley
Author, Chairman & Co-CEO, Man in the Mirror

Pitfall 2

Generational disconnect

*" . . . every generation has a conceit of itself
which elevates it, in its own opinion, above that
which comes [before or] after it."*

Margaret Oliphant – Novelist and historical writer

December 1964

Sixty-five-year-old Jack Belmont jerked the receiver from his ear and started to slam it in its cradle before stopping himself.

"Yes, son, I'm still here. But barely. I don't think you know what you're talking about. You've got ideas that are new to you, but they're not new. They sound great in a speech. Heck, I've made the speech myself. Many times. The trick is making changes that stick. You haven't been down that road and I don't think you have any idea what it takes.

"I've spent the last forty years building this business. I've learned more than I could ever get out of a book or seminar. I've had good people working with me, and we've learned together. One of these days I hope you can be at the top of the pile. I'm trying to figure out a way to make that happen."

Jack's intent was good. So was his 44-year-old son's. But the two perspectives were miles apart, and Jack's hope was growing dim.

Chapter 2

Listening to Understand
TOM CONWAY

"Oh, it is so frustrating talking to my dad. He never listens. He says he listens, but his actions speak louder than his words. He says he wants to hear my thoughts and opinions, but then he just goes off and does what he wants to do." The frustration came out of Jane's mouth as she shared with me her last conversation with her dad. She was exasperated, feeling misunderstood, undervalued, and walked over by her father.

Jane was not a 13-year-old child; she was the 26-year-old Executive Director of the family foundation. Jane had worked diligently to help the foundation establish fund-request protocols, all of which had been approved with only minor changes and embraced by the board members. She had felt good about her contribution and the board's approval.

Then Dad stepped in. Someone had approached him – off-line – and asked for a gift. Because the request failed to meet the guidelines, including a time deadline, it was denied. Dad, however, reversed the decision and approved the request over the phone. From Jane's perspective, it was just one more example of disrespect.

What is generational disconnect?

It is a failure to understand and appreciate differences. Age or stage-of-life gaps cause differences in perspective that add to the difficulty of understanding others. Feelings of disrespect often follow, leading to little communication of any depth as relationships weaken or even fracture.

Certainly there may be conversations or words exchanged between the generations, but there is no real listening and contemplating taking place. The children feel that their parents are not listening, and the parents often feel that their kids are being rebellious. This leaves both sides frustrated and discouraged.

The reality of generational disconnect

Generational differences exist in all families. Every generation develops its own style of expression, its methods for handling conflict, and even its own values.

Some parents don't understand how a cell phone can be used to access nearly anything in the world. Even tech-savvy parents are likely to feel that virtual connecting lacks sufficient depth to replace face-to-face conversation. Children, on the other hand, feel that Mom and Dad just don't get it and can barely turn on the TV without help.

Many times the older generation has not clearly communicated their values and why they have them. The younger generation doesn't understand, dismissing the values as old fashioned. When these generational differences are not addressed, they drift into a growing generational disconnect.

Why is it so hard for one generation to communicate to another? Here are some of the reasons we have observed.

"I know what I'm doing."

Dad (or Mom or Grandfather or Grandmother) is accustomed to command-and-control leadership. As the owner and president of a company he built with his own hands, people have been following Dad's orders for decades. He takes that for granted. Or in Mom's case, she has always run the family this way. She knows what is best for everyone.

Sometimes, as "King of the Hill," Dad leaves no wiggle room for any input other than his own ideas. When only Dad's ideas are considered, the children simply don't offer ideas, even if they are good ones. Generational disconnect results, and the family loses.

Mutual disrespect

For successful family conversations to occur, each person must have respect for the others and for their opinions. Parents and children typically lack sufficient respect for each other. Cries of "You just don't understand!" fill the hallways when parents don't do what their children request.

Parents generally expect children living under their roof and authority to be obedient, as they should. But when their expectation leaves little or no room for discussion, a disconnect is in the making.

Seeking to protect their children from some unpleasant consequence, parents may see questioning on the part of their kids as a sign of disrespect. Children, if old enough to reason, want to understand why they can't have it their way. Inability to question and hear reasonable answers not only shortchanges their learning process but also gets interpreted by them as disrespect.

If there is not mutual respect for each other's opinion, accompanied by an attitude of humility that listens to understand, conflict arises and generational disconnect deepens.

Past experiences

Many parents dismantle a lot of family capital while building financial capital. Whether spoken or not, "I'm doing this to provide for you and your future" is a typical parent message. The typical child message – deeply felt but less likely spoken: "Your work is more important to you than I am."

Think about the times when Dad promised he would show up for the ballgame or dance. After his no-show, the disappointed child hears that Dad got busy with a major account and couldn't make it. That's what the parent says, but the child, in childlike fashion, interprets it to mean that the customer counts and I don't. Dad says, "It won't happen again," but it inevitably does. These experiences are not easily forgotten. Or forgiven.

Busyness

Let's face it: we are living in the busiest time in recorded history. The prevailing attitude is that everyone is busy; if you're not, there must be something wrong with you. Our busyness leads us to make quick decisions because we don't have time to think or pray about the consequences of our decisions. The failure of either generation (all generations are guilty of this) to refuse to take time to think carefully and discuss their feelings and thinking can be devastating.

Overcoming generational disconnect

One of the most powerful tools in combating generational disconnect is humility. The Apostle Peter, writing to early church leaders, said, "... *clothe yourselves with humility toward one another, for God . . . gives grace to the humble*" (1 Peter 5:5, NASB). Humility frees us to listen with an attitude of respect and an expectation to learn.

The Apostle Paul puts it this way, "... *with humility of mind regard one another as more important than yourselves*" (Philippians 2:3, NASB). This attitude can be practiced by any generation. When a grandfather invites his grandson to express his opinion on a family matter – and actively listens – the self-esteem of the grandson skyrockets and the grandfather learns something he may have missed.

This does not mean that the grandfather yields his right to decide; it means that he is modeling humility and teaching responsible expression.

*Humility frees us to listen with an attitude of respect
and an expectation to learn.*

Evidence of an attitude of humility is active listening. Many stories are told to children. Later, as adults, many can remember details of stories they heard clear back in the first grade. Why? They were active listeners. New information was coming their way. Their minds raced with questions as they processed how the story fit into their world.

When was the last time you went to your adult child and asked for guidance on something? The same mind that asked you to read a certain story 50 times can probably explain something to you that would be just as revealing as your story was to them.

All generations have a responsibility to develop active listening skills. But it is particularly powerful when the family leader models them.

From abstract to practical

Humility and active listening are two of many components required for effective communication and healthy relationships – especially cross-generational ones.

We all have some concept of what humility is, and we generally think others are in greater need of its development than we are. It can be very difficult for us to perceive our own behaviors as deficient in humility.

Active listening, which is a behavior rooted in humility, should be easier for us to self-assess. But again, most people would rate themselves high as listeners even though their friends and family might rate them as average or below.

Skilled advocate "translates"

We often have difficulty matching our abstract concepts to our practical behaviors. This results in communication problems as difficult as those posed by different languages, and it is just one of many reasons that an advocate plays a vital role in important family conversations.

Because true collaboration requires considerable skill and discipline from all involved, most families never reach that level of communication. Skilled advocates, however, sense dysfunctional communication patterns early and defuse them before they sabotage the collaborative process.

Intergenerational giving and listening combined

Just before Christmas, a grandma and grandpa gave each of their grandchildren a brochure from an international adoption agency and $50 in cash to give to someone in need. At a family meeting some months later, the grandchildren were asked to share with the entire family where and why they gave the money and how they felt after giving it.

Each parent of each of the three families listened with great interest to what each child said about looking for needs and making the gift. The humility in each child was evident: the children knew they were "better off" than the recipients of their gifts, but they also recognized how much better they felt after making the gifts.

Their own desires for happiness were being met because of others. They were learning the ancient truth that generosity breeds happiness! In the words of author Criss Jami, "Old words are reborn with new faces."

But that's not the end of the story. As the family was together telling how each gift was made, and why, they gained more respect for each other. The mom and dad of each family were bursting at the seams to see how such a simple exercise brought them all together and enabled them to focus on something beyond themselves.

All three generations listened not only to each other within their nuclear family but also to the wonderful stories of their extended family. All three generations experienced a common joy as they focused on generosity, a focus which has since become a commitment to an ongoing mutual goal.

This exercise of generosity created generational connection – the antidote to generational disconnect – and brought joy to the entire family.

Questions to avoid this pitfall

1. How have you exhibited disrespect to the other generations in the family? How have you exhibited an attitude of humility?

2. Have your busyness and broken promises created a barrier in your relationship with anyone in the family? How might you ask forgiveness from that person?

3. How good are you at active listening? How would your family members rate you? (Consider asking them.)

4. What exercise can you think of that would bring your family together and allow each generation to connect better with the others?

5. What charity in your city could all family members rally around? What role could each generation play in helping this charity the most?

> *"The actions you take today not only impact you;*
> *they influence generations."*
>
> Dillon Burroughs –Founding partner of Activist Faith

Praise for unHeritage

The authors have provided an integrated path for those who seek to be wise as serpents and gentle as doves in the use of their finances for deeper purposes. The book doesn't tell people what to think or do, but counsels them to listen, learn, and act from their deepest wellsprings.

Paul G. Schervish
Director, Center on Wealth and Philanthropy at Boston College

It's about time we stopped the tail from wagging the dog. What good is it to inherit a pile of money if the family falls apart in the process? Too many estate planners have had their eye on the wrong ball – the obvious, easy one that promises something it can't deliver. This book is an eye opener.

Ron Blue
Founder, Ronald Blue, Author, Speaker

So many of us have our best conversations in our heads, when we think of what we should, want to, or are afraid to say to those who matter. CFC has written a deeply moving account of why it matters to talk openly to the ones you love, and to share your deeper feelings. This heartfelt book has the ability to move you to action.

Dennis Jaffe, Ph.D.
Family Researcher and Sociologist, Saybrook University

Pitfall 3

Husband/wife disconnect

*"Everybody claims they're being logical,
especially when they're in complete disagreement."*

Unknown

March 2008

JB (Jackson Belmont III), in his third marriage at 59 years old, took care to flatten his tone. "We already settled this in our prenup. Your kids are not my heirs. And even if they were, a pile of money wouldn't solve their problems."

"What makes you so sure, JB?"

"It hasn't solved mine." He wanted to soften his answer with a willingness to think about it, but there was no point in raising her hopes. The massive loans now supporting most of his assets were still his closely guarded secret.

"I don't want to argue about money," Amber said in a hushed tone. "But I don't think my kids are so bad."

"I didn't say they were. They're no worse than mine." He thought of 19-year-old Jackson IV and added, "Probably better. That's not the point."

Amber reached across the table and touched JB's hand. "I think you're being too hard on yourself."

"Maybe you're right," JB said with a conciliatory smile. But he knew better.

Chapter 3

Understanding and Valuing Perspective
TOM CONWAY

I've been in enough of these conversations to sense when sparks are about to fly. Doug's face was set as he and Susan sat across from me in our conference room. "My father set up trusts for my five kids, and they haven't had to work a day in their lives. I'm not leaving anything to them."

Before I could respond, Susan made an equally forceful statement. "I don't agree with that at all!"

Not exactly on the same page. Not even in the same book. Where do you go from here? How can two people who love each other as much as Doug and Susan do – and love their children as much as they do – have such different ideas about what is best for their children?

Dan and Holly were trying to decide what would be a proper inheritance for their two daughters. Dan thought a certain amount was adequate for these single girls in their late twenties. Holly's suggestion was four times larger than Dan's.

As if to prove the differences aren't gender based, Jim and Maryanne approached the issue from the opposite perspective. Jim felt they should leave a certain amount to their three children, and Maryanne went for a much lower number. And both felt they were right. What is behind the vast difference in perspective? Perhaps more important, how do you begin pulling these perspectives together?

Reasons for the disconnect

How does estate planning disconnect evolve? Certainly there may be many issues where a husband and wife are on the same page. They may be happy with their marriage, with their current lifestyle, with the common friends they have, but when it comes to making an important decision, they are not in alignment. Let's look at some of the possible reasons for misalignment.

Differing assumptions related to upbringing

Differing family backgrounds influence the way people see life. Those who grow up in wealth are likely to see an expensive lifestyle as normal. Naturally, they would expect the same for their children. This was the case for Holly, who had always shopped at the most expensive stores and thought her daughters were entitled to have that same privilege. Doug, on the other hand, had worked hard to develop himself and his business, and he saw the value in that. It grieved him to see his children growing up with money from a trust fund that killed their motivation to be productive.

Most parents want to protect their children from the tough times they had to go through, without realizing that the tough times helped them become the people they are today.

Many beliefs and attitudes grow out of early life experience. Most parents want to protect their children from the tough times they had to go through, without realizing that the tough times helped them become the people they are today. The nature of those tough times varies greatly, and without a conversation on upbringing and background, people are not fully aware of the resulting deep feelings they have. They are even less aware of their spouse's. This can make it very difficult for a couple to come to agreement.

Differing values

Your values are the things that you believe are important in the way you live and work. They play a significant part in the way you view life, generally determining your priorities. Whether you recognize them or not, they are there, and they are the measures you use to tell if your life is turning out the way you want it to.

Although it is challenging to examine how your emotions intersect with your thinking, this level of self-awareness is necessary to identify the values that motivate you. Once you recognize and acknowledge your values, you can make plans and decisions that honor them. Because many couples have not taken the time to write down their values and share them with each other, they can't understand why they view things so differently.

Understanding each other's values can really help a couple come to agreement on decisions. If you value family but have to work 70-hour weeks in your job, you will feel internal stress and conflict. If you value security, the perception that you don't have enough money will cause significant stress in your life.

Differing perspectives

Our perspective – the viewpoint we bring to any consideration – influences our perceptions. You have probably heard the expression, "Perception is reality." You may also have heard the expression, "My mind is made up; don't confuse me with the facts." Both of these statements help us understand how we sometimes fail to see the current reality of a situation.

Instead, we are satisfied that the way we see it is the way it is, and we are unwilling to entertain the thought that our view is distorted or incomplete. The situation with Doug and Susan is an example. Doug feels that because their children have always had a source of unearned income, they are not doing anything meaningful with their lives. It is his perspective, but it's not accurate; it's not the whole picture.

Four of Doug's children are leading meaningful lives and doing a good job with their families. One is not. Doug is focusing on the one and drawing a trend line from the attitude and activities of that one child.

It is his perspective, but it's not accurate;
it's not the whole picture.

Susan, on the other hand, is very connected to the children and doesn't see the negative impact on their lives that Doug sees. Her motherly instincts are to protect and provide for her children. Further complicating matters is that Doug doesn't want to talk about it.

Lack of understanding leads to loss of communication

When spouses don't agree on certain topics, they often avoid the subject. Though Doug and Susan would say they have a good marriage, they find it difficult to discuss their differences in an attempt to resolve them. Doug hates conflict and would rather suffer the pain of silent disagreement than the pain of confronting and talking about feelings. He knows that he and Susan are not in agreement about how to deal with their estate, but he feels that by avoiding the discussion they are keeping peace in the family. This false peace, however, can lead to devastating family consequences in the future.

Pride

All of us deal with an internal nature that wants our own way. We often feel that our way is the best way and that if everyone would just do as we say, or believe as we believe, the world would be a much better place. This pride can cause us to become defensive when we are challenged. It can also lead to a closed mind. The Bible uses the term "stiff-necked" for the people of Israel who wouldn't listen to or obey God.

The opposite of pride is humility. The Bible says that God is opposed to the proud but gives grace to the humble. To be humble means to be willing to listen to thoughts and opinions of others with an open mind. It means being willing to submit your own ideas to the scrutiny of others. So many conflicts in life can be resolved if two people approach the issue with a listening ear and an attitude of humility.

Solving the issue

So how can a couple resolve the issue of goal incongruity? Often they cannot do this alone. Their differences often bring on heated discussions that lead to anger, hurt feelings, shutting down by one spouse, and pain. And no progress is made. But the same couple can take steps to resolve these differences, steps that involve the help of an advocate.

The role of an advocate

An impartial advocate can have a huge impact on a couple that can't seem to agree. An initial step is to define the problem to be solved. The status quo – whatever default decision is in place – will have undesirable consequences. Bringing clarity to this current reality provides motivation to seek a solution that is at least incrementally better. Moving from zero percent agreement – Doug and Susan's current state – to 60 percent agreement is a vast improvement and a much stronger platform from which to build.

Writing your values

Often the advocate guides the family through a values discussion. This helps them understand why their spouse holds the position they do. People who have not had the benefit of a values discussion with an impartial third party often don't recognize the values upon which they are making their life decisions. Once they see and understand their values, they can be helped to see the ones that may be contradictory to their core beliefs.

The decision-making process

Walking a couple through the decision-making process outlined in Chapter 6 can bring clarity to a decision for both parties. In addition, it helps the couple understand their spouse's reasons for their feelings, enhancing communication between the two. A thoughtful advocate can help people prioritize their objectives, evaluate the alternatives, and make a decision.

Questions to avoid this pitfall

1. How might you benefit from a trusted advocate who can facilitate the issues you are struggling with?

2. How well do you think your spouse understands your family background and how it influences your thinking? How well do you understand your spouse's upbringing and its effect on their current decision making?

3. Have you ever taken time to write down your personal values and prioritize them?

4. Have you shared them with your spouse?

5. Have you discussed what values your children appear to have and how you might influence the development of their values?

Praise for unHeritage

Successful legacy plans pass both wisdom and wealth to heirs. This book, written by experienced wealth advisors, will guide head, heart, and spirit, as you make legacy decisions that will inspire your family for generations to come.

Phil Cubeta
The Wallace Chair in Philanthropy at The American College of Financial Services

Alongside my late brother Scott Fithian, I have spent my career counseling advisors on how to open the walls for family communication and collaboration related to Legacy. One of Scott's famous lines was, "Focus first on what your clients value, not the value of what they own." unHertitage provides the opportunity and structure for an awakening of what's possible in family wealth planning. I highly recommend unHertitage to families (and their advisors) who want to pass on their values as well as their valuables.

Todd Fithian
Managing Partner, The Legacy Companies, LLC

There are few books that offer the opportunity for a "short read" while including ideas, information and opportunities to last a lifetime. This is one of those books; I highly recommend you make it a priority read.

Barbara A Culver
Founder, Connect-Gens, Cincinnati, Ohio

Pitfall 4

Lack of next-generation leadership

*"Leadership: The art of getting someone else
to do something you want done
because he wants to do it."*

Dwight (Ike) Eisenhower

June 1959

Jack, now sixty, slipped quietly back into bed at 3:15, hoping not to wake his wife. She didn't stir.

Thirty seconds later, without a trace of grogginess in her voice, Doris asked, "Where have you been?"

"I couldn't sleep, so I took a sleeping pill."

"That doesn't take an hour."

"Do you really want to talk about this now?"

"Might as well. I've been awake, too."

Jack sighed. "It's the same old thing. Jack junior thinks he's ready to run the business, but he's not. I'm trying to figure out how to deal with it."

"I know it's not easy mixing family with business," Doris said. "I'm glad you're working on it. If something were to happen to you, we'd be in a mess the way things are right now."

"Do you know something I don't?" Jack asked, surprised by Doris's response.

"Of course. I know lots of things you don't."

"I mean about Junior and the business."

"No, but I'm concerned about the family. Little JB is a real handful."

"What do you expect? He's only ten."

"I know. I'm probably worrying about nothing. I just don't want to see the family unravel, and sometimes it looks pretty shaky."

"I'm sure it'll sort itself out," Jack said. "It's the business that's keeping me awake right now. That's *my* concern."

Chapter 4

Preparing the Next Leaders
STEVE GARDNER

"What kind of leader am I?" It was a rhetorical question Grant had asked of himself, and he barely paused. Pointing to the acres of production facility below his office window, he continued spilling his guts to Derrick, a legacy advocate who had come highly recommended but whom he had known for only a short time.

"It's such a paradox," Grant continued. "No one survives decades of taking risks and growing an enterprise to this size without being a halfway decent leader. I'm not the greatest, but I'm probably in the top twenty percent. We've gone from manual assembly to crude automation to sophisticated robotics, and I've been able to lead the necessary changes all along the way. Why is leading a family any different?"

"I suspect you know the answers," Derrick said. "Why do *you* think it's different?"

"For starters, building my company wasn't like herding cats. For the most part I was leading a coalition of the willing. I paid people to do what they were supposed to. If they refused, I replaced 'em. Not always pleasant, but it's just part of the cost of doing business. I can't do that with family. At least not without a LOT of cost, if you know what I mean."

Derrick chuckled. "And the emotional cost is a lot harder to deal with than the dollars."

"There was a time when I wouldn't have thought so," Grant said, "before I had any dollars."

"And probably before you had kids," Derrick added. "I'm guessing they inherited your strength, but they don't use it to pull in the same direction."

"That's putting it mildly," Grant answered. "Sometimes it feels like they're all pulling in opposite directions. And hard enough to tear the whole thing down."

"What whole thing, the business or the family?" Derrick asked.

"Either. Both. Depends on the day."

"Which are you more concerned about?"

"That's a good question. I think at this point I'm more concerned about the family. A healthy family could survive a dying business, but if the family dies, I wouldn't get much pleasure out of my business success."

Derrick didn't speak immediately, letting the weight of Grant's last statement settle fully. "I really appreciate your perspective," he said finally. "You've put a lot of thought into this. It's a common problem that revolves around family leadership – past, present, and future. You've led the business successfully, but you're not sure you've led the family so well, and you fear that the family will further disintegrate when you pass from the scene."

"That's it," Grant replied.

A healthy family could survive a dying business,
but if the family dies, I wouldn't get much pleasure
out of my business success.

Derrick continued. "It sounds like you've come to the conclusion that you need to put the same kind of effort into getting your family aligned that you have put into getting and keeping the business aligned."

"Exactly," Grant said. "I'm just not sure the same kind of effort can get it done. Family is a different dynamic."

"Yes, it is, but you've faced different dynamics in the past, and you've been able to adjust your leadership style enough to get by. More than get by – you've been very successful. The principle is similar. How would you describe a successful family leader?"

Grant thought for a moment. "I think it's someone who can get most of the family to do things that are in their best interest and help them see enough benefit in it that they decide to keep it up themselves."

"Good," Derrick said. "Sounds like casting a vision and helping people create a path to it. It really is a lot like business, because even in business you can't force customers to buy from you."

"Now there's a connection." Grant said. "You just said you can't force customers to buy from you, but we're not talking about customers. We're talking about family. As soon as you said it, it hit me. I've been thinking of family more like employees than customers. Maybe that's part of what needs to change. The kinds of assumptions I make about employees don't apply to customers. They take quite a different approach."

"I think you're on to something," Derrick said. "What do you do to attract and keep customers?"

"We don't take them for granted, that's for sure. We create campaigns and go after them."

"Do you have people directing the effort and seeing to it that specific responsibilities are covered?"

"Sure. It's too important to leave to chance. Things don't get done by themselves." A smile broke across Grant's face. "But that's what I've been expecting, isn't it? I've been thinking that family members, like good employees, should see what needs to be done and get on with doing it."

I've been thinking of family more like employees than customers. . . .
We don't take [customers] for granted, that's for sure.
We create campaigns and go after them.

"Seems logical," Derrick said. "And it's the way virtually every entrepreneur thinks. But a little tweak in perspective can make a big difference. You generally get a lot further if you lead family members more like customers than employees – especially the adults who aren't already fully committed to a family legacy. As they get involved with defining outcomes, you'll begin to see a next generation of family leaders emerge. Creating some specific family roles will help you maintain your 'customer' base."

"I get the customer analogy," Grant said, "but what kind of family roles are you talking about?"

"Whatever roles are needed to support the family's chosen outcomes. Some families have a Chief Connection Officer, a Chief Emotional Officer, a Chief Events Officer, a Chief Educational Officer – whatever it takes to execute a plan and maintain progress toward their outcomes. Having a passionate person on point with these components of family identity and unity is vital. Otherwise, they are likely to slide into oblivion."

"But what if you don't have any chosen outcomes? We don't have any of these things yet."

"No problem," Derrick said. "Clarifying outcomes is best done in collaborative discussion with as many family members as possible. Some won't want to engage at this level at first, but don't be discouraged and put it off. It's too important."

"How do you start?" Grant asked.

"Begin brainstorming with whatever customers you can attract and build from there. It's usually best to start by discovering the family's shared values. That's an easier discussion to get people to agree on. Your family values then become a runway for other important discussions, including outcomes."

"So, start by identifying values before attempting to define outcomes," Grant repeated as he thought through the logic of the sequence.

"Yes. Values are more abstract and lead to concrete outcomes. Families generally have difficulty trying to agree on outcomes first, but outcomes naturally flow out of values."

"That's an interesting distinction you make between abstract and concrete. In my experience, some people are better at one than the other."

"Important point," Derrick said, nodding in agreement. "Some family members think more conceptually and some think more concretely. That's a good thing, because both are necessary if strategy is going to become reality.

"As you brainstorm desired outcomes," he continued, "you'll discover that some ideas are higher level – broader and more conceptual. Others will be more specific and concrete. Make sure you value all suggestions. Then at an appropriate stage in the discussion, begin the process of identifying themes, the overarching categories into which specific outcomes could be placed."

"Examples?" Grant asked.

"Sure. One common theme is discovering and developing the strengths of each individual family member. Clarification involves answering What, Why, and How questions that move toward greater detail. For instance, what does "discovering strengths" involve? Why should we do it? How can we do it? What does "developing strengths" involve? Why should we do it? How can we do it? Gaining clarity and agreement from general to specific is necessary for implementation."

*Some family members think more conceptually
and some think more concretely . . . both are necessary
if strategy is going to become reality.*

Grant's excitement began to build, but as he thought of specific family members, he felt a sense of hopelessness invade his shiny new vision. "Any suggestions for attracting customers in the first place?"

"Let me give you a three-minute overview. First, it helps to think of family members as having two identities: a relational identity and a team identity. The first identity is legal membership by right of birth or marriage. The second identity is team membership by right of choice.

Team members adopt the family's chosen values. They choose to prepare and participate. They strive to meet the standards of the team and to contribute to its success."

Grant smiled. "I never thought of it that way before. Two identities – legal membership and team membership – one by chance and the other by choice."

"Yes," Derrick continued. "Everyone in the family has the legal identity, but that alone doesn't produce alignment. And everyone in the family has the opportunity for team identity if they want it."

"Such a simple concept," Grant said. "But I can see how we could work toward a culture of intentionality with a setup like that. We would be proactively writing the family story we want instead of passively accepting whatever happens."

"Exactly. 'Team' members have additional responsibilities and expanded benefits. Communicating this concept in broad terms creates interest in what the additional responsibilities and expanded benefits might be. But you can't answer with specifics yet, because they don't exist until you define them together."

"Defining things together sounds great," Grant said, "except that we can't seem to do anything together right now."

"I'm not suggesting that it will be easy, but you can definitely do it. Leading a family is like attracting customers in business. It takes the same kind of relational effectiveness. You focus on providing safety and trust, enabling every member of the family to understand that their voice and participation have value. Three 'S' words describe what family members must feel as they participate." Derrick wrote on Grant's white board.

- Security: feeling safe to assert themselves; feeling encouraged to take first steps
- Success: feeling that they are part of a family that will work together toward a bright future
- Significance: feeling that what they contribute will make a difference

Derrick continued. "These three 'S' words go a long way toward building a team environment that draws members in and makes them want to stay. When that environment exists, families rarely have difficulty managing their wealth, because the problem is rarely the money; it's the people. Good character and good attitudes are the basis for healthy family leaders from generation to generation."

Grant nodded. "I've learned that one the hard way. If attitude isn't at the top of your hiring criteria, you can end up with a bunch of skilled professionals who undermine each other."

"Then you've got the basic concept," Derrick said. "A lot of estate planning gurus emphasize developing financial management skills. We don't disagree with that for family members who are so inclined, because it is an important team function. But we emphasize that all family members should develop emotional intelligence and the skills of decision making and relational effectiveness. These are foundational to the life quality of every member as well as the family unit."

*Relational effectiveness . . . provides safety and trust,
enabling every member of the family to understand
that their voice and participation have value.*

Questions to avoid this pitfall

1. How does the value of aligning your family compare to the value of aligning your business? How do the two require similar proactivity but differing tactics?

2. What kind of relational and developmental outcomes do you want for your family?

3. What leadership roles might your family create to accomplish these outcomes?

4. How can you engage your family in "What, Why, and How?" discussions that increase buy-in and create unity?

5. What guidelines do you have to help you maintain an atmosphere of Security, Success, and Significance for all family members?

Pitfall 5

Wayward child

"I have no greater joy than to hear that my children are walking in the truth."

3 John 1:4

April 2014

Nearing the hospital, JB (Jackson III) continued to ask himself, *How have we gotten to this place?* Every question he raised about how his 25-year-old son could be in such a predicament led to additional questions – none of which seemed to have satisfactory answers.

I just can't figure out what's going on in his head was the single conclusion to which he consistently returned. *If he knew the fortune was gone, I would understand it, but he doesn't have a clue – at least not yet. What does he expect from life? What's he not getting?*

JB parked near the ER and ran to the entrance. It never occurred to him that the last two questions he had asked himself were more than a decade late.

Chapter 5

Preparing Heirs
BILL HIGH

What is it about our kids that prompts such great emotion – from elation to depression? Certainly, there is no greater joy than to see our children flourish and no greater agony than to see them wander from our values and our beliefs.

A few years ago our foundation had a large event – more than 1,000 people in attendance. As part of the program, we wanted to diversify our lineup of speakers, so I asked my daughter Jessica to speak. At the time, she was a 19-year-old college freshman.

She had to leave school early that day, drive a few hours, and with very little preparation time step onto a stage with bright lights, cameras, big screens, and a large audience of sophisticated achievers. But my daughter stepped to the microphone and talked with poise, humor, and emotion. She was captivating. In the aftermath, many told me that she was the best part of the program.

I had to agree. I was bursting at the seams.

Contrast that with a lunch I had a few years ago with my friend Steve. His shoulders were slumped and his voice, halting, as with moist eyes as he talked about his son.

Sam had been such a good kid through the early years, full of activity and excitement. Sports, drama, church, and youth group had filled his days. But something happened along the way. Sam lost his way, lost interest in what had previously excited him.

By college, he was wayward – into destructive behavior and disconnected from the family. With stumbling words, Steve told me that he would gladly give up his great career, big house, and all the trappings of success if only he could have his son back.

Irony: neglecting the "soft" side

The greatest irony in family estate planning: spending countless hours on the "hard" side of assets while giving lip service to the "soft" side of people development.

A man recently contacted me about reviewing his estate plan. He told me that he was at the "end." He had completed it and didn't want to look at it again but had decided he wanted me to give it one last look.

The documents – tax returns, financial statements, LLC forms, family limited partnerships, and multiple trusts – filled an impressive binder. I could see why he was tired; it represented a staggering amount of time and legal work.

His kids, grandchildren, and future grandchildren would be financially set for a long time. He had tied up all the financial and legal loose ends quite well.

But sadly, I saw little of the soft side of the man and his wife in those documents. I saw nothing on the story of the family, nothing to help guide future generations by showing them how they got to this point. What did it cost them to get here? What were their pain points? What were their joys?

Within those documents, there were no compass settings – no values statement, no mission statement, no future vision. There was no cohesion – only the money. And money more often divides than it unites.

The tendency in estate planning is to prepare legal documents that transfer financial wealth without preparing our children for true legacy. What does preparing our children for true legacy mean?

Preparing children for true legacy

Life is often a blur in the child-raising years. In the same timeframe that we are raising kids, we are building our careers. And frankly, some of us tend to do a better job of building financial wealth than "family wealth." Much of what our children learn is left to chance: whatever they observe along the way.

When things finally settle down a bit, the children are graduated, off to college, or even absorbed with starting their own careers and families. How do we prepare them for the next phase – for truly understanding family wealth?

What is family wealth?

In his book, *Family Wealth*, James Hughes discusses the importance of human capital that includes the following outcomes – ideally for all family members:

- They are thriving.
- They have a strong sense of purpose, passion, and calling.
- They have a strong sense of work ethic and character qualities like integrity, honesty, and compassion.
- They have strong interpersonal relationships both within the family and externally.
- They understand that life does not revolve around them but that instead they are part of a greater whole, a greater cause.
- They have spiritual grounding.
- They are generous.

These are big ideas, which go way beyond transferring financial capital. They go to transferring intellectual capital, social capital, emotional capital, and spiritual capital as well.

Here's the tricky part. Generally speaking, financial capital is easy to transfer. It is more transactional in nature, and any competent professional can structure the transaction.

But to truly prepare heirs takes something more than a transaction. Preparing financial and legal documents is a transactional task. Preparing heirs is a relational process. Relationships take time, and slowing to the speed of relationships isn't easy.

Good relationships require time.

I've seen many families as they get ready to travel out of the country. They rush around preparing legal documents and making massive decisions about wealth transfer in a matter of days. They sweep through like tornadoes, leaving a wake of paper to administer hasty decisions that affect kids and grandkids for generations. That is not legacy.

Relationships take time, and slowing
to the speed of relationships isn't easy.

The Grand Canyon was not formed by a tornado. It was formed by the constant attention of wind and water to rock over a long period of time. It's an awe-inspiring sight. And so it is with relationships.

Good relationships require intentionality.

That's the way lasting legacy is formed. It's time spent with children with intentionality – making sure they understand our story and that we understand theirs. It is time spent repairing relational damage that is unintentional but inevitable. It is making sure they are healthy, thriving, and feeling fulfilled – or at least have a pathway to get there insofar as it is within our power.

Value of an advocate

Families often benefit from an advocate, someone to help them navigate the soft side of legacy planning, someone who is experienced at helping families discover their shared values, someone who is clearly on their side in the big picture.

I know that may sound self-serving, and it is. But it is also true. Great achievements and great financial wealth are sometimes the result of a hard-driving, get-it-done, take-no-prisoners kind of founder/leader. Collateral casualties may be dismissed as a cost of doing business, but they aren't dismissed easily when they include spouses and children.

When that hard-driving leader suddenly shows up and wants to talk legacy, he simply can't do it. It may well be perceived as "just another project." The kids don't want to participate or they have limited enthusiasm because they know they won't be heard.

Not long ago, I was consulted by one of those hard-driving business guys. He'd built quite a business, which was operating in several countries. Now in his latter years, he wanted to work on "legacy." When I met with his kids, they responded with a sarcastic "Yeah, right!" They didn't think he really wanted to listen to them. They were glad for the presence of a third party to help the conversation along.

Giving together creates unity.

In light of this framework, one of the best tools I've found to bring families together is giving together. Structurally, that may take the form of creating a foundation or a donor advised fund. But practically, it simply means doing some giving together.

Giving is the great equalizer. We'll talk more about this in an upcoming chapter, but suffice it to say that giving prompts conversations and values on a neutral plane that everyone can participate in regardless of age or experience.

And children who learn to give alongside Mom and Dad are less likely as adults to see their parents as uncaring and selfish – labels often attached to parents by estranged children.

Investing in legacy

So what do you want when you think about your heirs – great joy or great agony? It will take great effort to achieve the former. It must go beyond estate documents. Estate documents are a part, but they really should be guided with the influence of all forms of capital – intellectual, social, emotional, spiritual, and financial.

To achieve lasting legacy, a family will invest deeply to ensure that their children and grandchildren and subsequent generations understand:

- The family values
- The mission of the family
- The vision for the family in the future
- Their unique family story and their own place in it
- That the health of each family member – true capital – is maximized

Although it takes time, the view from the canyon is far more fulfilling than the view from the tornado.

Questions to avoid this pitfall

1. As you consider your own family legacy, how would you evaluate the health of each family member – spouses, children, grandchildren?

2. What practical steps can you take to instill the human capital in your children that will prepare them for inheriting financial wealth?

3. Consider your estate documents. How well do they reflect something beyond just a financial transfer of assets? What can you improve?

Praise for unHeritage

This book is a must-read for both successful families and their advisors. It covers the whole spectrum of those areas families need to act upon if they hope to maintain their legacy of family heritage intact for future generations.

Johnne Syverson
President, Syverson Strege & Company (Past President of AiP)

unHeritage combines scriptural truths with practical wisdom to illuminate 11 pitfalls that can ensnare the most well-intentioned parents and grandparents. Your family will be the beneficiaries of the time and energy you devote to integrating unHeritage's best practices for family flourishing.

John "John A" Warnick
Attorney, Founder of the Purposeful Planning Institute

Passing money and assets to the next generations is easy. Passing the true wealth of a family is much more difficult. unHeritage condenses some of the key issues within the context of real life stories. Although every family is unique, these concepts and principles touch us all. From the 11 pitfalls to the solutions and facilitation needed to avoid them, everyone interested in leaving a positive legacy will benefit from reading this book.

Rod Zeeb JD, HDP™
CEO, The Heritage Institute

Pitfall 6

Indecision leads to inaction

"Plans fail for lack of counsel,
but with many advisers they succeed."

Proverbs 15:22

September 1975

"But I'm not ready to make those decisions yet," Junior protested to his wife when she brought up the "trust" discussion again.

At 53 years old, Junior had finally gotten the CEO role on Jack's seventy-fifth birthday, but Jack's delay was not due to indecision. He just didn't want to give up control. Jack Belmont rarely second-guessed any of his decisions. Moving quickly and boldly was one of his greatest assets, and sometimes, one of his greatest liabilities.

Junior, having suffered consequences of his father's hasty decisions, chose the opposite extreme. Confronted with having to make the tough calls, he would drag his feet, citing complex variables that defied simple interpretation.

His chronic uncertainty led to indecision, inaction, and decline. Signs of decay in both the business and the family screamed for strategic intervention, at which Junior typically responded with another round of his favorite strategy: delay and hope for the best.

"When will you be ready?" Betty prodded.

"I'm not going to pull an arbitrary timetable out of my hat," he insisted. "When the time is right, I'll know it."

Betty drummed her fingertips on the table and said nothing. *He'll know it when he's looking up from under the sod,* she thought.

Chapter 6

Making Decisions – Process and Action
TOM CONWAY

Dan and Cathy sat in my office deep in meditation. I asked, "What do you believe would be an appropriate inheritance to your three children that would be a blessing to them and not a curse?"

As they pondered this question, Dan mentioned a number, and then Cathy mentioned a number. It was not the same number. They discussed the reasons for their differing conclusions, but neither was ready to embrace the partner's answer.

John and Sally had a similar dilemma: "Should we keep the family farm that has been in the family for generations or should we sell it because none of our children want to be farmers?"

When people wrestle with decisions that have significant implications on the future of loved ones, it is often a hand-wringing experience. It is not unusual for people to pay significant sums for legal documents that they never subsequently sign.

Many times, uncertainty leads to inaction. They do nothing, not realizing that indecision is a default decision with consequences of its own. Why do people procrastinate? Why do they not take action even when they know the current reality is not what they want?

Perspective

Many people don't realize that they already have a plan – one of the government's choosing and not their own. If they pass on to eternity today, some existing plan will kick into gear, and it may not be what they want.

I recall saying to a client, "Frank, you have a plan right now, and at your admission, it is not a good one. If you walk out the door and have a heart attack, your existing plan will be implemented. I know you don't know what the future holds, but creating a plan that covers 60 percent of what you want puts you 60 percent ahead of where you are today. In two or three years you can revisit the plan and maybe move it to 70 or 75 percent of what you want. You may never hit 100 percent, but with prayer and proper guidance, you will be a lot closer than you are today."

When people make decisions that will impact the lives of others, it is important to realize that today's decision need not be their final decision. Because of extended lifespans today, there is a very good chance that they will revisit their plan and change it. Most decisions are not irrevocable.

Many people don't realize that they already have a plan – one of the government's choosing and not their own.

Former CEO and business psychology author William B. Given, Jr. gives this sound advice. "When possible make the decisions now, even if the action is in the future. A revised decision is usually better than one reached at the last moment."

So what keeps people from making these decisions? Consider these factors.

Lack of clarity

One factor is lack of clarity on what the individual or couple wants to do. The decision is sometimes compounded by lack of clarity on what they believe God wants them to do.

When people are unsure of the objective they want to accomplish, they have no confidence in making a decision. Closely aligned with lack of clarity is that people do not take the time to seek God's guidance.

Peace often comes after time spent in quiet prayer and meditation around a decision. *"And the peace of God, which transcends all understanding, will guard your hearts and your minds in Christ Jesus"* (Philippians 4:7).

Fear

Fear is another factor that handcuffs decision making. Fear that they will make the wrong decision. Fear that they will disappoint God or others with their decision. Much of this fear is tied to emotional uncertainty. What will they or others feel about the decision they are making?

Ron Blue, in his book *Splitting Heirs,* speaks of three questions people should ask themselves as they make wealth transfer decisions.

Question 1: What is the worst and what is the best thing that can happen if you transfer wealth to your child?

Question 2: How serious is it?

Question 3: How likely is it to occur?

The answers to these three questions can bring great clarity to a decision.

Inadequate information

Sometimes people don't make decisions because they don't have enough information. In the wealth transfer arena, people are often uncertain of what their children will do with the wealth they entrust to them. Will they be good stewards or managers of what they are given? Will they squander it frivolously?

The uncertainty of related circumstances may also cause a person to hold off on a decision. If a company is negotiating a pending sale, it may be unwise to make a decision until they know whether the sale will go through.

Personality

Couples generally differ in personality type, with one likely to make quick decisions while the other wants more time to think – the intuitive versus the analytical. One may embrace risk while the other desperately wants to avoid it. One is likely to favor logical thinking while the other is more concerned about feelings and possible consequences for the people involved.

Larry Burkett, a wise author in the area of finances, said "God did not give you your spouse to frustrate you, but to complete you." Take time to be patient with your spouse, giving the needed time to achieve peace around the decision you are making.

Don't know how

Many people do not have a decision-making process they trust. What do I mean by a process? I mean a step-by-step decision-making process that leads to a decision they can live with. The decision they come to may not be the perfect one, but it is the best alternative at the time based upon the information they have.

A decision-making process

There are many factors that go into making a decision, but having a process to filter decisions through can be very helpful. A decision-making process I learned and have used over the years with clients has ten steps that begin by submitting the entire process to God. *"Do not be anxious about anything, but in every situation, by prayer and petition, with thanksgiving, present your requests to God"* (Philippians 4:6).

1. Pray for guidance. Prayer and meditation can often help you gain clarity around a decision.
2. Define the decision. What is the question you are trying to answer – the problem you are trying to solve?
3. Clarify your objectives. What are the decision criteria? What are you trying to accomplish with this decision?
4. Prioritize the objectives. What are the non-negotiables around the decision? What are the must-haves versus the want-to-haves?
5. Identify your alternatives. Are there other ways to get to the same objective?
6. Evaluate the alternatives. What are the facts you are dealing with? What is the current reality?

7. Make a preliminary decision.

8. Assess the risk. What could go wrong here if I make this decision?

9. Make the decision.

10. Test the decision over time for future improvement. Ask yourselves, do we as a couple still agree with this decision? Do we have peace about it? Is it still the best of all the alternatives we have considered?

Conclusion

Remember that some plan is already in place, whether it is the result of your conscious decision or merely the default because of indecision. Ask yourself: Do you really want to live with the current reality? Engaging an advocate is often the most efficient and effective way to break out of indecision and inaction.

Questions to avoid this pitfall

1. Are we clear on what decision we are wrestling with – what problem we are trying to solve?

2. Have we given time and prayer to the decision or are we in a hurry?

3. What is keeping us from either making the decision or acting on it?

4. Who might help us think through the alternatives and the consequences of the decision?

> *"Man does not simply exist,*
> *but always decides what his existence will be."*
>
> Viktor Frankl – Holocaust survivor

> *"If you always do what you've always done,*
> *you will always get what you've always got."*
>
> Henry Ford – Industrialist

> *"Trust in the Lord with all your heart,*
> *and do not lean on your own understanding."*
>
> Proverbs 3:5 (NASB)

Pitfall 7

Lack of a succession plan

"Hope is not a strategy."

Rudy Giuliani, New York City Mayor

December 1973

Jack Belmont, now 74, abruptly stopped pacing and whirled to face his legal counsel. "Of course I know what I'm going to do with the business! When I'm ready to step down, I'll do what any good father would do. Turn it over to number one son to run. I'm just not ready to step down yet."

"Glad to hear you're not ready to turn it over yet," the attorney said. What he thought but didn't say was, *and Junior sure isn't ready to take it yet.* "Have you considered other options?"

"Yes, but my mind is made up. End of discussion."

Within the year, Jack got some unwanted medical news, turning up the timetable on his "plan."

"At last!" Junior said to Betty, "My chance to run the show is finally in the official plans. You'll be Mrs. CEO soon."

Within two years, Junior began to suspect how ill-suited he was for the CEO role. Propped up by strong, supporting leaders loyal to Jack's dream, the business continued to prosper. For a while.

Chapter 7

Planning Your Inevitable Exit

JERRY NUERGE

Randall began his business a little over thirty years ago with a good idea, very little money, strong drive, and a lot of guts. Most weeks have seen him investing sixty to eighty hours of hard work, although he is quick to add that most of the "hard" has also been fun. Now the business is worth hundreds of millions, and Randall has a problem: his doc says he needs to slow down and reduce his stress level before it incapacitates him.

Dilemma

This has created a dilemma for Randall: he can't figure out what to do with the business. All of the normal options have downsides he hasn't been able to resolve. And, frankly, he hadn't given it much thought until now.

Whenever he'd heard the term "succession plan," he had assumed it applied to public company corporate executives or serial entrepreneurs who loved the create-to-sell cycle. But why would it apply to him? The company was his baby, the one he had nourished through rough waters and sharks fighting it out in the world of competition. He'd had to believe in this kid when everyone else was going in a different direction. More than once he had put his family's finances on the line, risking everything to seize growth opportunities.

How in the world did I allow this
guaranteed dilemma to sneak up on me?

For the first time, Randall was facing the inevitable: a massive transfer was about to take place, and he had been too busy to plan for it. "I've always believed in business plans," he told me, "even if they weren't formally written. I've had contingencies for problems that had only a ten percent chance of occurring. How in the world did I allow this guaranteed dilemma to sneak up on me?"

Endgame preparation

It's a good question. Many legendary leaders, folks who built America into the greatest economic machine known to mankind, have blown their endgame. So what are some key factors to look for in a successor when it's time to step aside?

Education

Many entrepreneurs abbreviated their formal education as they pursued their dreams. Their passion drove them relentlessly, focusing their energy on the challenge at hand. They made mistakes, paid the price, and learned through the school of hard knocks.

But now, the stakes have risen and the complexities of staying competitive in a global market continue to increase. Mistakes that were formerly valuable learning experiences could now be fatal for the business. A solid education is no longer a luxury; it's a necessity for any successor in a major business. Do your children qualify?

Experience

Owners of a closely held business generally gain their experience on the job. They grow up with the business – alongside it as the business itself grows up. The next generation(s) grow into the business, often without realizing the extent of work and sacrifice they will need to exercise.

The founders had no manual showing them what to do next; they had to figure it out as they went and develop good judgment in the process. Expecting a child or an inexperienced outsider to step in and have this kind of judgment bestowed upon them is asking the impossible. High hopes soon give way to frustration.

Rarely do owners mentor their successor for five to ten years in the CEO role before deciding to step down. They assume that their children, by virtue of growing up around the business and having some involvement in it, will rise to the occasion and suddenly exhibit their leadership chops. Are you setting yourself (and perhaps your children) up for the shock of your life with this kind of approach?

Emotional attachment

We've already noted the deep emotional attachment founders have to their work. It's their baby! Successor CEOs do not usually come with this deep emotional attachment, but it builds within them as they hear significant stories of the business.

It is not Superman success stories that create emotional attachment; it is the stories that reveal the founder's fears, challenges, failures, vulnerabilities, and commitment to problem solving and growth.

Founders need to answer questions like these with stories that capture the drama of past challenges.

- Describe your three most exhilarating events. What breakthroughs did you discover?
- How many times did you have to regroup and start over with a different or tweaked game plan to finally hit a breakthrough?
- What are the biggest lessons you learned when a project was not successful?
- How did you transition from negative to positive in the process of getting to a breakthrough?

Stories like these, when documented, become an integrated piece of the business culture and foster a closer emotional attachment for successors.

Work ethic

Most closely held business owners have an excellent work ethic. If they are older they may have backed off somewhat, but they know what it took to keep the business on track in the early years. It is natural for the next generation in the family to assume that they shouldn't have to work that hard. After all, they experienced the missing dad or mom many times.

But when the next generation thinks they can coast through their duties and merely show up because others will get the work done, two huge consequences occur. First, respect is lost among fellow employees. Second, the business loses its sense of direction: no one is truly committed to getting things done.

Good preparation includes challenging potential successors with projects that require hard work. Their response will help you judge their ability to earn the respect of others and keep the company headed in the right direction.

Some in, some out

Many owners face emotionally charged decisions when some children work in the business and others do not.

- How do you treat the children equally when this occurs?
- Are there ways to transfer assets to children on an equal and fair basis when some are in and others are out?
- What traps might you unintentionally set that could result in sibling rivalry after your passing?
- How do you make the "outside" children just as vital to family culture and harmony when they have different careers?

Although there are general principles that apply to these decisions, there are no one-size-fits-all answers. An experienced advocate can help you determine the unique application that answers your specific situation.

Visionary path

One of the most crucial elements business owners must deal with is the visionary path for the company. After leading for decades, they know the business and industry inside and out. But rarely have the potential leaders from the next generation been deeply involved in discussions dealing with the future. How do you host such discussions?

We scheduled a retreat with one of my clients who had one son in the business and one who had left it for a different career. Both sons and their wives gathered to discuss how the closely held business would be operated once Dad was no longer involved.

As we facilitated the discussion, it became clear that the son who had left the business had no desire to own stock or come back and work in the business in the future. Mom and Dad were now able to plan how they would include this son in a fair way that allowed harmony to prevail.

Sooner rather than later

Randall, the business owner without an exit plan at the beginning of this chapter, inadvertently increased his stress level at the very time he needed to decrease it – simply because he had been in denial regarding his own need for a succession plan. Procrastinating didn't avoid the inevitable; it just made it harder and hastier.

It could have been worse. A couple of years of below-average profits are far better than a fire sale, but if he had it to do over . . . .

Questions to avoid this pitfall

1. How far along are you in determining the specifics of your own succession plan?

2. What will you do to resolve the issues (or competing values) that have kept you from completing your succession plan?

3. How long do you intend to mentor your successor?

4. What next steps should you take now?

Pitfall 8

Misunderstanding how to treat heirs – equally or uniquely

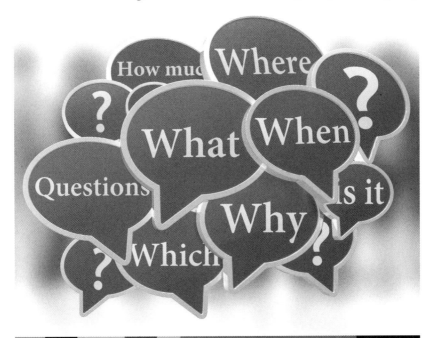

"Love them equally, but treat them uniquely."

Ron Blue – Financial author

April 1988

"JB can't screw it up any worse than Junior has for the last fourteen years!"

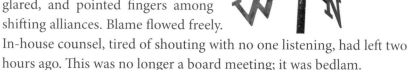

Nine sets of couples – two generations of siblings and their spouses – alternately screamed, glared, and pointed fingers among shifting alliances. Blame flowed freely. In-house counsel, tired of shouting with no one listening, had left two hours ago. This was no longer a board meeting; it was bedlam.

JB (Jackson Belmont III), at 39, hadn't expected any crack in the deadlock but had hoped for a chance to strut his stuff. The company had been in decline for years, and the family's patience was running out on Junior.

Jack, the entrepreneurial patriarch, gone for fourteen years now, had never imagined how his simple formula would backfire. "Leave the business equally to all the kids and let 'em duke it out. Number one son runs it, if they don't run him over. They'll learn."

Unfortunately, they hadn't learned. Jack's idea of equal treatment had seemed fair enough at the time, but it hadn't accounted for widely varying degrees of business sense. Democracy had become anarchy, and the anarchists had no solution but to hope the next guy in line could produce a miracle.

Chapter 8

How Much to Children?
BILL HIGH

It's one of the biggest questions I get from thinking families. How much should I leave my children? Many make the default decision and leave them everything. But that approach is beginning to change for a variety of reasons.

1. As lifespans increase, primary beneficiaries may be in their sixties or older – a stage in life when financial needs are often diminishing.

2. Similarly, as the age of inheritance has gone up, the "fruit" of the children is more readily known, resulting in a reluctance to leave money to irresponsible children.

3. As wealth has increased, there's a reluctance to leave the entire fortune to children as well as a desire to make sure children retain an incentive to work.

Nevertheless, the decision on how much to leave children is filled with emotion. That emotion springs from a desire to love our children, have them love us, and a desire to treat them fairly.

Consider George. He was a classic self-made business guy. He came from a small town and moved to the big city to find more work and better opportunity. He started working construction until he figured out he could do just as well on his own. So he started his own company. The business grew, expanded, and survived the tough times.

I met George at a time when he was tired and ready to pass on the business. His daughter was the operations manager and, for all practical purposes, ran the business. His biggest problem was his only other child, his son. He had never worked in the business, lacked his sister's intellect, and worse, was a spender. George loved his son but was afraid to give him a lump sum, let alone an interest in the business.

Or consider Martin. Like George, he started his company out of necessity. Martin crafted a reputation for honesty, paying on time, and doing quality work. The business grew and allowed him to employ two of his sons. But his third son had no interest in the business and became an artist. His fourth child, a darling daughter, had struggled the most with a variety of addictions.

Yet years before, as part of his estate planning process, Martin had been encouraged to make each of his children equal shareholders in the family business. Martin knew he needed to reward the two sons in the business but was at a loss on what to do with his other son and daughter.

Unfortunately, there is no single best approach to answering the question of how much to leave to children. There are principles that can guide us, however.

1. An inheritance is a good thing. The Bible is clear that leaving our children and grandchildren an inheritance is a good thing. Of course, one of the first principles to realize is that an inheritance is more than just money.

It includes the passing on of values, virtues, character qualities, work ethic, great family memories, and great family stories. All of these combine in the family narrative. The goal should be to leave a complete inheritance, not just money.

An inheritance is more than just money.

2. Favoritism is a bad thing. Perhaps one of the most destructive things in families is when a parent or parents play favorites. The classic story of Jacob and Esau from biblical times is a haunting reminder. Their father favored Esau, a strong hunter, a man of the field. Their mother favored Jacob, who stayed in the tents with her. The favoritism produced strife among the brothers such that Esau wanted to kill Jacob.

But what is favoritism? I think this is perhaps the lost question. Favoritism is bad when it springs from an apparent bias for no apparent reason. This is frustrating to children because they can't do anything about it, and it simply makes them question their own value.

Favoritism is bad when it springs from an apparent bias for no apparent reason.

3. Provide equal love and acceptance and equal opportunity. Unlike favoritism, the goal of parents should be to provide equal opportunity and love. Love your children equally. Provide them equal opportunity.

Give them the same opportunity to succeed and thrive in whatever areas of interest they may have. In the context of a family business, each of the children can have equal opportunity to join and grow.

Notably, in Matthew 25, Jesus called his servants before him, and while he gave them differing amounts of capital, they each had equal opportunity. Each servant had the same opportunity to invest and grow the capital received.

4. Distribute according to need, responsibility, and performance. Here's the dividing line. We don't want to favor one child over another. We want to give them equal love and opportunity. But the simple truth is that our children will vary in how they handle the responsibility.

Some children will shine with responsibility. Some will only partially embrace the opportunities they've been given. And some will reject or squander their opportunity.

As a general note, if the kids normally handle their opportunities responsibly and faithfully, there's certainly good grounds to distribute equally. Inequality of distribution usually arises when there is a greater disparity in the handling of resources and responsibility.

Matthew 25 is once again instructive. In calling his servants to him, Jesus recognized the differing responsibility levels of his servants. They received differing levels of capital based upon their ability to handle the responsibility. The reward was in line with their faithfulness in executing on the opportunity.

5. But what about those who choose another opportunity? It is perhaps easier to address a child who refuses to take responsibility than it is to address a child who simply chooses another opportunity. In the context of a family business, it is not uncommon for one or more children to work in the business while one or more may choose not to work in the business. The question is, how do you treat those who choose not to work in the business?

Applying the above principles, if the child who chooses not to work in the business demonstrates responsibility and the ability to handle wealth, consider treating that child equally with those who are in the business. However, this equality may have a twist: it can be most beneficial to award company stock to the children in the business, while awarding non-business assets to the child not in the business.

6. Consider how much should be passed on compared to giving to charity. Parents can make reasonable, prayerful, discerning decisions on how much they want to pass on to their children. The answer may be 100 percent, 50 percent, or even 10 percent.

As those determinations are made, an option that is not often brought up by planners is that families should also consider how much they want to go to charity. They can use a variety of means to pass gifts to charity: private foundations, donor advised funds, or direct gifts. But a key element in the process is to ask the question of how much to give to charity in the same way they ask the question regarding their children.

The considerations contained here are not absolutes, but they provide some good guidelines for discussion. Each family is unique. The "how much" question deserves to be explored in a broader and deeper context, involving both husband and wife and taking into account the feelings and opinions of each.

Questions to avoid this pitfall

1. How are you avoiding favoritism as you consider how to provide for your heirs?

2. How do you describe the difference between equal opportunity and love on the one hand and differing financial bequests on the other?

3. What criteria have you established to guide the amount of your bequests?

Pitfall 9

Lack of beneficial modeling

"Children have never been very good at listening to their elders, but they have never failed to imitate them."

James Baldwin – Social critic

July 1926

After dinner on Sunday, Jack and his young family settled on the front porch to watch the storm clouds in the distance. Jack winked at Doris and subtly nodded at four-year-old Junior standing next to him with an identical pose.

Jack folded his arms, and Junior followed suit. Jack unfolded his arms and extended one to the railing, leaning against it. Junior did the same. Jack yawned and sank to the floor, sitting cross-legged. Ditto. Doris could barely disguise her grin.

Ten years later, the grin had faded. "Jack," she said more than once, "I'm concerned about the example you're setting. Won't you go to church with us?"

"I go."

"Christmas and Easter."

"I go more than that."

"You went four times last year."

"You're keeping count?" Jack asked.

"Junior already resists going. He says if it's not important to you, it's not important to him. But I think it *is* important. For all of us."

"Okay, I'll talk to him," Jack said. "But right now I can't afford the time. I've got a business to build. I write the checks, you put them in the plate. Everybody should be happy."

Chapter 9

What's Your Role?

RYAN ZEEB

Modeling and parenting go hand in hand – for good or ill. Some of the best parenting advice I've seen over the years identifies three high-level roles:

1. Set an example.
2. Provide guidance.
3. Make wise decisions.

In this short chapter, I want to describe the parental focus I have adopted based on my experience as an advocate for high-net-worth families.

I can't tell you how many families I've worked with that said their number one desire is to have a lineage of family members who had a close relationship with Jesus Christ. Most want their children to have careers that fulfill them, and most certainly desire a good family name, but the number one objective I've heard from Christian families is that each family member would build a close relationship with Christ. Most parents don't know how to be proactive about this without forcing "religion" on their children.

When my wife was pregnant with our first child, my pastor asked me if I knew what my job as a father was. I knew lots of people who say you never really know what you're in for when it comes to marriage and parenthood until you experience it yourself. So I gave a comprehensive, honest answer: I had no idea.

Thoughts went through my head of raising the next generation's leader. Certainly I would need to provide finances, discipline, and mentoring along with supporting my wife through the journey. The more I thought about it, the more I hoped my wife had a better idea of what we were getting into than I did.

I'm so glad my pastor had some very simple yet sage advice. "Remember that your job is to prepare good adults, not good children – adults who leave your home with the resources to be successful, independent of you." I began to understand what he was saying when our own two-year-olds threw fits in really inconvenient places like restaurants and church.

Your job is to prepare adults who leave your home with the resources to be successful, independent of you.

Yikes! The stakes just went up. Preparing them to leave was a bit of a new concept; I had never heard anyone position it that way before. Most parents I talked to were dreading the day their children would leave home. Many said "Enjoy them while they're young, they grow up fast." It seemed counterintuitive to focus on the parting, the dreaded venturing from the nest, but I've come to appreciate the wisdom of this counsel.

What would they need to be prepared and have the resources to be successful?

The more I thought about it, the closer I moved to the conclusion of so many of my clients: I wanted my children to become disciples of Jesus Christ. Having a close and personal relationship with Jesus covered many of the necessary bases for being successful.

What, then, is the parents' role in guiding their children to become disciples? I know I can't force my children into a relationship with Christ. And the path to discipleship certainly takes the Holy Spirit to move in their lives.

Fortunately, the Bible has a lot to say about our role as parents. Since this topic could be its own series of books, let's narrow our focus to a few verses from Deuteronomy 6 that outline three simple steps.

Step 1: Love God fully.

"You shall love the Lord your God with all your heart and with all your soul and with all your might" (Deuteronomy 6:5, ESV).

Why does the Bible always bring us back to the condition of our heart? Because, at least as far as I can tell, the only reason God created earth and humans was for us to be in relationship with him.

So, the first step is a self-check. Jesus said to go and make disciples. The implication of Deuteronomy is that I can't make a disciple unless I am one. The question, then, is: Am I a disciple – do I love God fully? I cannot pass along something I do not possess.

I've come to learn that discipleship is a process rather than a destination. A principle I see over and over in Scripture is the necessity of focusing on my own relationship with Christ before thinking about someone else's. Therefore, if my desired outcome is for my children to be disciples, I need to lead the way. I've got to be one myself – with all my heart, soul, and might.

Step 2: Know God's Word.

"And these words that I command you today shall be on your heart" (Deuteronomy 6:6, ESV).

Not only are we commanded to love the Lord our God, we must know him and know his commands. Preventable ignorance isn't part of the equation.

The second part of the Great Commission – after going and making disciples – is teaching them to observe all that Christ has taught us.

Since I can't impart something I don't possess, if I want my children to know God's commands, I've got to know them. Part of what it means to love God is to obey him, and that means investing time and brainpower to know him and his Word.

There is no other way. That is the design, and it is on purpose.

Step 3: Communicate God's Word.

"You shall teach them diligently to your children, and shall talk of them when you sit in your house, and when you walk by the way, and when you lie down, and when you rise. You shall bind them as a sign on your hand,

and they shall be as frontlets between your eyes. You shall write them on the doorposts of your house and on your gates" (Deuteronomy 6:7-9, ESV).

What strikes me in these verses is how continuous the process is. We are to teach, talk, observe, and proclaim what it means to know and love God. This isn't a one-time gig or a once-a-week thing. This is all the time, when I'm awake, when I'm lying down, inside and outside of my home.

When I get to heaven, one of the questions I want to ask God is why he didn't make the journey of following him a bit more of a progression. Maybe I'll describe the "Baby-Step" method from the movie *What About Bob?*

Seriously, I'm already starting to feel like a failure; there is no possible way I can do this on my own. And then I remember God's purpose. God set the bar this high so we are REQUIRED to depend on Him.

My job is to model this to my children: model a posture of returning to our Savior whenever failure occurs, because it will occur.

*God set the bar this high so we are
REQUIRED to depend on him.*

So that's it? Does the Bible say anything else about my role as a parent? Yes, more than we can cover in this brief chapter. But I'll leave you with a parable from Jesus himself.

"'A sower went out to sow his seed. And as he sowed, some fell along the path and was trampled underfoot, and the birds of the air devoured it. And some fell on the rock, and as it grew up, it withered away, because it had no moisture. And some fell among thorns, and the thorns grew up with it and choked it. And some fell into good soil and grew and yielded a hundredfold.' As he said these things, he called out, 'He who has ears to hear, let him hear'" (Luke 8:5-8, ESV).

In this parable, the seed is the Word of God. I'm going to suggest there are multiple layers of depth to this parable.

We are to prepare our own hearts into good soil. We nourish our soil with God's Word, healthy relationships, and prayer.

As parents, if we follow the prescription in Deuteronomy, the fruit of the Spirit will be part of our lives. This will help us prepare the soil in our children's hearts, and when the moment is right, the Holy Spirit will move in their lives.

My job is to cultivate the soil of my children's hearts, diligently teaching and modeling for them a posture of reliance on Christ, who is the eternal Word.

It's hard to imagine that God loves my children more than I do, but He does. And the purpose of this life is to continue in relationship with Christ with all our heart, soul, and might. My job is to cultivate the soil of my children's hearts, diligently teaching and modeling for them a posture of reliance on Christ, who is the eternal Word.

"Whoever has ears, let them hear" (Matthew 11:15).

Questions to avoid this pitfall

1. What can you do to implement the steps of Deuteronomy 6?

2. Who else can assist in cultivating your children's hearts?

Pitfall 10

Lack of generosity

"They are always generous and lend freely;
their children will be a blessing."

Psalm 37:26

December 1965

Jack Belmont walked with JB, his 16-year-old grandson, toward the front door of the dealership. Christmas lights blazed from the roof, lighting up the volunteer bell ringer stationed at the Salvation Army collection pot.

"God bless you. Merry Christmas," the bell ringer said to every one passing by.

Jack pulled a fifty-dollar bill from his wallet, handed it to JB, and pointed at the collection pot. JB's eyes widened. "All of it?"

"What do you think? Tear it in half?"

JB slid the bill through the slot and felt a warm sensation in his chest. "How will it get used, Grandpa?"

"I don't know. Some of it might buy food or shelter for homeless people, I suppose. Why do you ask?"

"Well, it feels good to give, but I think it would be even better if I knew how it helped somebody."

"That's good, JB. Someday maybe we'll have time to think about that stuff. But for now, we've got cars to look at."

Chapter 10

Teaching Them to Be Generous
BILL HIGH

Generosity is far more than just giving money; it is about a way of life. It is about being willing to give of our time, our talents, and our treasure. And it is one of the greatest tools in teaching family legacy.

Frankly, you can fail in a lot of areas, including financial and estate documents, but if you succeed with generosity you can cover a multitude of sins. The Psalmist got it right: the righteous family is generous, and their children become a blessing.

Tom's story

Tom is a talented musician. He majored in music, but he suffered from serious introversion. He had to brace himself just to call the pizza delivery guy – it was too much interaction with someone he didn't know. But somehow, despite his introversion, Tom ended up in a sales career.

His musical mind gave him the ability to understand complex financial products and investments. He was also able to find a way to orchestrate the right conversation with potential clients. These, along with a disciplined sales approach, enabled Tom to top the sales charts in his company. His gratitude to God led to generous giving.

But God needed to do some work in Tom, and he orchestrated an unexpected plan. In the wake of Tom's success, a disgruntled former employee looked for a way to take down the company. He sued Tom, and this led to charges from his licensing boards. Websites were created to talk about Tom's unethical practices. His entire career appeared to be in jeopardy. In this process of humiliation, God was teaching him humility – that it really was not all about Tom – it was about his dependence on God.

As a result, Tom had multiple choices to make in all of this uncertainty. One of them involved giving. He and his wife talked about whether they could continue to give at the levels they had given before the charges were filed. Because of their dependence on God, they realized that they needed to – and most importantly wanted to – keep giving at unusually high levels.

Ultimately, the charges were dropped. Tom's name was cleared, but the story didn't end there. Because Tom and his wife had elected to continue giving, they'd gotten involved with an organization running orphanages in Haiti. They took a number of trips there, including one with their eleven-year-old daughter, Anna.

Anna's story

Anna encountered a level of poverty she'd never experienced before. Yet in the midst of their poverty, she saw Haitian children smiling and singing with joy.

Upon returning to the United States, Anna was moved to action. She asked God what she could do about the poverty she had seen. She realized that, like her father, she'd been given the gift of music.

She created a music CD, using her gift of playing the violin and singing. Dedicating the proceeds to building orphanages in Haiti, in just a few years Anna had raised over $100,000.

The great equalizer

Why does generosity create such great family legacy? The answer is quite simple. Generations connect over shared experiences, and generosity is an equal-opportunity experience. A grandchild can't really share the experience of the grandparent's role in running a business but can share equally in the joy of giving and meeting someone's needs.

Think of it this way: if Anna went to her father to talk about financial products and sales, his twenty-plus years of experience would far outmatch her eleven years of elementary school math. However, when Anna approached him with her passion for orphans in Haiti, her personal experience could not be denied. It was hers. Her desire to respond to the need she saw was just as valid as anything her parents had experienced.

Generosity is the great equalizer.
Everyone's experience is valid.

When a family sits down to talk about giving, they can talk about people and organizations they've come into contact with. Each person can talk about emotions, thoughts, and reactions to needs they see around them. As that discussion ensues, the opportunity to talk about values surfaces.

Generosity discussions lead to discussions about important values.

I know one father who gathered his family to talk about a significant giving opportunity that would require them to choose from among several organizations. But before choosing, the father was able to articulate the values he hoped would guide their choice. In particular, he wanted to make sure they chose an organization that would go beyond mere social service to also share the message of Jesus from the Bible.

It was a watershed moment in the family. They'd never heard him speak so openly about what motivated him. Yet it was a safe place. None of them felt like a set of values was being crammed down their throat personally. To the contrary, these values were being talked about in reference to an organization. The values discussion gave them a frame of reference for how they should choose.

Giving allows us to talk about values in reference to an organization or a need. It is much easier for teenagers to discuss values – and evaluate them – in this context. What they often fear or resent is messages being preached at them, the "you" messages such as "you should do this" or "you shouldn't do that" or "you should believe."

Give a Benjamin Day

I recently participated in an unusual Christmas lunch with a group of men enjoying a "Give a Benjamin Day." A Benjamin, of course, refers to a $100 bill. So before lunch, about twelve of us split up to "Give a Benjamin" to a person we felt a nudge by God to give to. It was a fun morning. And by the time we gathered for lunch we had a great assortment of stories.

Lessons learned best are lessons practiced.

There was the guy at the bus stop, and when we pulled up and whipped out a bill, he responded by saying, "Wow! This has never happened to me before!" There was the double-amputee war veteran who used the cash for a train ticket to get home. There was the grandmother who could now afford to have her grandchildren for a Christmas dinner and the man who could now afford to pay an overdue bill. The stories went on.

The idea of "Giving a Benjamin" worked so well that I tried it with my kids. The stories we got back were equally inspiring. But most importantly, I heard my daughter say, "I want to be about generosity." Lessons learned best are lessons practiced.

Getting started

How do you get started with teaching generosity? Some of it is simple, beginning with the universal need to learn to share. Many people reading this may have started by teaching their children to give out of their own allowance or earnings. Some may even have set up piggy banks for giving, saving, spending. These are all great ideas.

Spontaneous giving

I like to extend the idea to some of these spontaneous acts of generosity. I have a good friend who regularly carries around a $100 bill to give away to someone he sees in need. He's done this so often that his children expect it, and they get to participate in it. This idea of spontaneous generosity teaches them the idea of being ready to give.

Structured giving

I have many friends who've set up foundations or donor advised funds to do their giving as a family. I have another friend who actually set up donor advised funds (giving accounts) from which his grandchildren could give.

The idea behind using a structure to give is that it formalizes giving, making it a good expectation and creating a "place" for the family to give. Regular times can be set for discussions about giving. This is balanced against spontaneous generosity. It also gives the opportunity for children to participate in larger giving decisions than their own earnings allow.

Beyond money

But clearly, giving extends beyond mere money. It includes giving yourself, your time, your passion. Kathy started small with Operation Christmas Child.

Operation Christmas Child provides shoe boxes of basic necessities like toothpaste, school supplies, and toys to children around the world. Kathy engaged her children in the endeavor. But she wanted more. So she started increasing her goal on the number of shoe boxes she would fill.

Each year the number grew, and her children participated not only in the act of buying supplies but also recruiting others to give. The number of boxes grew so large that Kathy had to recruit teams of volunteers to pack them. Last year Kathy and her children packed over 1300 boxes.

Here's the deal: no matter where they go, no matter what they do, or how much material wealth Kathy's children may obtain, they'll never be able to get over experiencing a house stacked full of boxes and supplies for someone else. That's legacy prompted by generosity.

Questions to avoid this pitfall

1. What practical steps can you implement to prompt giving discussions among your family – children, grandchildren, great grandchildren?

2. As you consider giving, contemplate acts of generosity you've experienced personally – whether giving or receiving. What was meaningful about them?

3. What values do you believe should guide your giving? How could you discuss them with your family as you consider giving together?

Praise for unHeritage

unHeritage is definitely the lighthouse for protecting your family and wealth for generations. Leading experts bring their learnings along with real-life stories from their ultra-high-net-worth clients to provide us with a roadmap for transferring true wealth between generations. This book is a must read for anyone interested in legacy planning.

Enzo Calamo
Attorney and CEO, Lugen Family Office Inc.

Don't be fooled by the simplicity and readability of this book – the principles get right to the heart of the matter. The question – how to equip and train families to live together successfully while using the totality of their wealth to greatest advantage – is an issue worthy of our deepest concentration. These authors have identified the key questions and provided straightforward answers that advisors and families alike would be wise to study and apply.

Scott Farnsworth, JD, CFP©
President, SunBridge, Inc., President, Main Street Philanthropy, Inc.

unHeritage provides a clear and concise roadmap for finishing well by choosing the positive alternative to the mistakes so many families wished their parents would have avoided.

David W. Holaday
Wealth Design Consultants, LLC

Pitfall 11

Undeveloped family story

*"Unhappy families are
conspiracies of silence."*

Jeanette Winterson – Author, Professor

October 2006

"Hey, Belmont. Hold up a minute."

Jackson IV glanced at his watch. Three minutes until the bell for history class. *I can't wait to get out of this dump,* he thought. "Yeah, Deke, what is it?"

"I just got an assignment for the school paper. I need to do a piece on a local family that typifies the entrepreneurial spirit. You're the first one I thought of."

"No way." Jackson said, resuming his stride toward class.

"What do you mean? It'll be easy. Two pages and I'll do the writing. All you've got to do is tell me about your great grandpa and a little about your grandpa and old man. Piece of cake."

"Nothing to tell," Jackson grunted. "Never met the first one. Grandpa died seven or eight years ago. I get the impression he was a loser. And there's nothing interesting about my old man. Find yourself a real family."

"Come on," Deke pressed. "At least think about it. Maybe I could interview your dad."

"Good luck with that," Jackson said, stopping at the door. "He would know more than I do, but he cares even less – if that's possible."

Chapter 11

Your Story and *Family Brand Equity*

JERRY NUERGE

*"Unhappy families are
conspiracies of silence."*

Jeanette Winterson – Author, Professor

Does Jeanette's quote cause you to begin asking yourself questions like it did me? I immediately began to wonder. How happy is my family? How much do we communicate about what matters most to us? How much do we self-reveal? How far along are we on the journey toward greater emotional health and fulfillment because we really know and care about each other?

Mere information isn't enough. Facts, laws, and even principles are cold and weak until they are infused with meaning that includes the passions of real life: the longing, the trying, the failing, the regretting, the learning, and the trying again – this time with more experience and better judgment. This is the fabric of our life, and the stories that recall it are crucial to the building of any lasting legacy.

Consider:

"The world is shaped by two things – stories told and the memories they leave behind." – Vera Nazarian

"Stories have to be told or they die, and when they die, we can't remember who we are or why we're here." – Sue Monk Kidd

"Your story has the potential not just to transform you, but it has the capability to serve a greater purpose and to impact the lives of those around you." – Ben Arment

"Power consists [largely] in deciding what stories will be told."
– Carolyn G. Heilbrun

The disconnect

Only one percent of the families I've worked with over the past 40 years had made any attempt to capture their family story and leverage its power. I can't help but wonder at the disconnect, especially in this high-tech world of instant global research and connection.

Write down the first names of your
great-grandparents from memory.

Here is a quick way to discover for yourself how well your family has handed its story from one generation to the next. Write down the first names of your great-grandparents from memory. I'm not asking for ancient history or lots of detail – just three generations back, and simple first names. Unless you've done a genealogy study recently, this probably will be a struggle.

When it comes to the most important lessons of life that forge family identity, ninety-nine percent of families rely on a verbal handoff from one generation to the next. How well that worked in the old days, I can't tell. But I know that it's not working today.

We've become a generation of detached islands without a memory connecting us to the mainland. The orienting and preserving power of our family story is lost by the third generation if it is not written down or digitally saved.

Families are forever.

The Center for Family Conversations maintains that families are forever. Just as God created each of us to be unique individuals, together we comprise unique families. Our family history is loaded with backstory that provides the context in which we perceive life and make the decisions that forge our future. The vitally important good and bad lessons learned along the way need to be captured well enough to pass to the next generation.

"We can tell people abstract rules of thumb which we have derived from prior experiences, but it is very difficult for other people to learn from these. We have difficulty remembering such abstractions, but we can more easily remember a good story. Stories give life to past experience."

– Roger C. Shank

Assets, in spite of preservation efforts, generally fail the three-generation test. Most estate plans give great attention to financial assets, with the goal of preserving them from tax erosion. Unfortunately, very little attention is given to preserving them from the most serious erosion – lost family identity and virtues.

The fact that only ten percent of these assets make it to the third generation is not the result of inferior legal documents; something else is missing.

The general pattern

1. Generation one creates the assets, often at family sacrifice.
2. Generation two inherits the assets without hard work or a connecting message that embodies what it took to build the assets and how they should be managed. Many of them feel justified living off a shrinking asset base because of real or perceived childhood deprivations from a workaholic dad.
3. Generation three has even less of a work ethic, developing an increasing attitude of entitlement that requires greater withdrawals to maintain a lavish lifestyle.
4. Generation four, who may not even know the first names of the asset creators, has little or nothing left but entitlement.

The common disconnect from the family story is further complicated by modern culture's mobility, with children often living hundreds or even thousands of miles away from Mom and Dad. Their busy lives make it a challenge just to maintain social visits over holidays and vacations. Who is going to raise their hand and successfully capture the family story?

The Center for Family Conversations has learned that most families in this environment simply procrastinate and do nothing other than create the legal documents that will mitigate tax erosion. These documents, unveiled at the passing of parents, are sometimes the first realization the children have regarding anything connected to the wealth of the family. Often shocked and fearful about what to do next, they don't know where to turn for counsel.

A better way

Imagine that your great grandchildren could instantly write down your first names and tell the stories of the three most exciting things that happened in your life. Imagine further that each story contained a life lesson that could help guide them to a positive result in their own family. Now their attitude becomes a feeling of gratitude rather than entitlement, a desire to pass along a rich heritage rather than the bitterness of bad luck.

These combined stories are your family's narrative – the family story. It typically intersects with another vital piece of your family's identity and culture: your values. Author Donald Miller says, "A story is based on what people think is important, so when we live a story, we are telling people around us what we think is important."

Your family story also intersects with the virtues you strive to exhibit, most of which are linked to your faith journey. Faith, whether expressed subtly or obviously, often provides much of the "why" behind the values of wealth creators. Family narratives that include a faith legacy are enriched and strengthened because of the long-term nature of an eternal perspective.

Family brand equity

The values, the virtues – including the faith perspective – and the story together create a "cord of three strands," something that Solomon says in Ecclesiastes 4:12 "is not easily broken." We refer to this three-stranded cord as *family brand equity.*

The values, the virtues, and the story together create a "cord of three strands" – family brand equity.

Family brand equity exists – good or bad – whether you are aware of it or not. Regardless of what it is at the moment, you are the key to making it better and stronger.

I said in the first chapter that values define the family, virtues build the family, and the story describes the family. Let me amplify that. The story does more than just describe. It also plays a role in defining and building, because it is the stories that stick in young minds – actually, in minds of all ages.

As important as values and virtues are, they often remain abstractions until they are given the combination of concrete detail and powerful emotions that characterize stories. Stories have been used through the ages to not only describe truth but also to teach it, make it memorable, and give it an emotional attachment in the hearer.

So how do you pull this off? You might say, "I'm just not a natural storyteller. The whole idea seems like a huge mystery to me."

If that's your response, it might comfort you to know that you're not alone. But that doesn't solve the problem. As with most problems, you'll need to push through some discomfort – as you did with learning to ride a bicycle – to gain a basic skill.

My grandchildren love to hear stories of when their parents were little. Sometimes when I ask them, "What would you like to hear about today?" they ask for the story about their dad beating the older neighbor kids in a bicycle race or the time their mom was hanging by her hair from the swing and had to be rescued by her brother. And I say, "You've heard that one several times. Are you sure you want to hear it again?" I know the answer: of course they want to hear it again! So, I smile and tell it again.

Asking good questions is like priming a pump for interesting stories – whether you ask them of yourself or others. At the end of this chapter we have a list of questions to spark your imagination.

Fortunately, every journey begins with a single step. Awareness is the first step: awareness that your family's story is vitally important and awareness that help is available. The Center for Family Conversations is comprised of advocates who regularly assist families in this as well as in facilitating the other components of *family brand equity*.

There are multiple ways to capture the family story. Some begin by writing memories and thoughts. Some conduct interviews and record the responses. Begin with something simple. As you see the benefits for yourself, you may choose to progress to something on a grander scale. But get the ball rolling in a way that makes it attractive for other family members to join in. www.befamily.com and www.thestoryofalifetime.com are two sites dedicated to helping families record small stories that build the family story.

Get real.

The best family stories are captured by someone in the family who loves and leads by example. Love drives a desire to benefit the family, both present and future, and inspires the humility to be transparent.

God gives us the example with biblical characters – including the heroes – realistically depicted with assets and liabilities, good judgment and poor, times of obedience and disobedience. What we don't get (or need) is an airbrushed PR piece.

Since everyone is fallen and no family is exempt from failures, a good family story doesn't attempt to present family members as gifted exceptions to the world of imperfect people. In order to identify with them and benefit from them, we need to see their struggle to gain victory in the universal challenges of life.

Sample questions to help you get started

Don't attempt to tackle all of these – certainly not in one sitting. And don't wear out your welcome if you're interviewing someone. These are merely samples, springboards from which you can create your own list.

1. What kind of house did you grow up in, and what was the old neighborhood like?
2. What was your favorite holiday as a child, and how did your family celebrate it?
3. If your great-grandchildren knew your first name, what would you want them to say about you?
4. If you were to start recording your family story today, who in your family would you talk to first? Why?
5. How did you learn about the most impactful character in your family?
6. What tragedies or failures in your family history might hold a story of resilience or lessons learned?
7. What are three of the most exciting events in your life? Why did you choose those?
8. How would you describe your greatest achievement so far?
9. How would you describe your greatest disappointment? How did you handle it?
10. Have you had any "failed" relationships? What have you learned about yourself as a result?
11. What leaders or mentors (that you know personally) have had the greatest impact on your thinking and life? Why?
12. What are three of the most important decisions you ever had to make?
13. What role in life has been the most fulfilling for you?
14. In what ways would you like to grow personally in the next year?

From an Elephant's Mouth

We asked Daryle Doden, founder of Ambassador Steel and Ambassador Enterprises, a few questions regarding what he has learned related to legacy as a businessman and father of five grown children.

And in case you're wondering, the choice of the word "elephant" is not ours. It's Daryle's self-description as a high-net-worth person who sometimes feels like the object of a hunting safari – an easy target for anybody who wants something.

This interview format provides an example of how a few good questions can prompt the sharing of valuable thoughts and feelings that would otherwise remain unspoken – lost with the passing of their host.

Abbreviated interview with Daryle Doden

Daryle, how did you connect with the Center for Family Conversations?

Creative visionaries have made me a lot of money over the years. I'm not one, but I can spot them. So, when Jerry Nuerge showed up at our offices, I was pretty sure I had spotted one. That's exciting for me, because it gives me a sandbox to play in – bringing a strategic perspective that creative visionaries need.

Knowing that Jerry had some good ideas, I asked our senior executive team to see if we could help him develop those ideas along the lines of family legacy and managing the opportunities and problems associated with transfer of wealth. We sponsored symposiums that resulted in the formation of the Center for Family Conversations.

As I think of their potential value, I see a platform for facilitating family conversations relative to legacy and generational transfer. I see the Center providing tools for people who engage in those conversations as well as for the professionals who assist them. I am personally less concerned about financial transfer – whether to ministries or heirs – and more concerned about providing an avenue and opportunity for people to fulfill God's purpose in their life.

Now that the sale of Ambassador Steel is history, what do you anticipate for the next phase of your life?

We are living in a time when we as business leaders can have a significant impact. I recently read a comment by Billy Graham about his expectation that the marketplace is going to have a redeeming effect on culture. That's what I've always hoped for.

I'm grateful that God has given me good gifts that my family and others have been able to enjoy and that he has entrusted me to be a steward of his resources. Our goal should be to create more than we consume. Second and third generations – and beyond – often have trouble with this because they were born with higher consumer expectations along with the capacity to fulfill them. In other words, they didn't have to invent the income wheel by looking so hard for a need to fill.

What do you envision your grandchildren and great-grandchildren saying about the family in the future?

That they have a godly legacy they want to pass on. Our godly legacy – our fortune – is a living faith, not money. I really want to emphasize a faith lived out daily as opposed to mere belief in a set of doctrines. Faith that is not demonstrated by actions is a sham, whether through hypocrisy or lack of self-awareness.

I also hope they continue to communicate the truth about one of the most subtle yet pervasive dangers of money: it allows us to live out our natural self-centeredness. If not handled with true humility, it can be a character-eroding cancer that quietly destroys us.

What do you do to foster family identity and unity?

We enjoy extended-family vacations together as well as multiple holiday functions. We're enlarging a lake cottage that will serve as an additional focal point for family gatherings and fun. Behind the design for the cottage are the driving themes of faith, values, virtues, and relationships.

We also have a weekly telephone conference call in which we share concerns and pray for one another.

When you talk about the godly legacy you want to preserve for future generations, how do you see your influence in that?

We strive to live godly in front of our children. As parents, our primary tool is influence, and the most powerful influence is modeling. If we really believe something, we'll live it out. If we do, it tends to stick downstream. If we don't, our children sense the disconnect and reject our empty words.

Figuring out how money plays into parental influence is an ongoing challenge, because there is a fine line between using money to influence and using it to control. Every time we make a decision about giving money to our children or grandchildren, we are looking for the same outcome: we want to open doors of opportunity for greater positive impact in their world. To the degree they see themselves as part of the river and not a dead-end reservoir, additional resources are likely to be healthy rather than toxic.

What are your thoughts about transferring principles that are more important than assets?

What we are most passionate about transferring to our children and beyond is something far more precious than money and physical assets: it is valuing relationships above everything else. That's what it means to live out the Great Commandment, to love God with all your heart, soul, mind, and strength and to love your neighbor as yourself. It's having a heart for God and a heart for people.

How difficult is it to get the Family Story written?

It's difficult for several reasons. But first let me qualify this: when you say "Family Story," I assume you don't mean some kind of PR piece that attempts to put a good face on a bunch of imperfect individual stories. Since a family is a collection or community of individuals, any accurate composite would be a summary of individual stories. The thing that can make it cohesive – beyond the obvious blood connection – would be shared values.

Let me describe it this way. As the wealth creator/patriarch figure, I could write a story that focuses on what I value and what I've tried to accomplish. It would include many accounts of failing forward, learning, and relearning valuable lessons. That's one kind of family story that could be inspirational and instructive as it lifts up virtues and worthy objectives.

Our purpose is to take a group of individuals who are bound by blood through no choice of their own and forge an enduring affinity group bound by conscious commitment to shared values.

Part of our composite family story is a family covenant that includes a statement of faith, a listing of family values, covenant affirmations, and a provision for annual renewal. Each member who wants to participate in the trust signs an agreement. The trustee does not investigate to enforce performance; the agreement operates on the honor system. Family members are free to choose whether they want to commit to the values in the agreement. A choice not to sign is not a choice to divorce the family, nor is it irrevocable.

The family values our family has chosen to live by include:

1. Authenticity/openness/vulnerability
2. Learning and growth

3. Integration of faith and life
4. Personal morality and integrity
5. Hard work/productivity
6. Excellence in all things
7. Relationships
8. The church and community

Some might question whether signing the family covenant should be a condition for participating in the trust. Our purpose is to take a group of individuals who are bound by blood through no choice of their own and forge an enduring affinity group bound by conscious commitment to shared values.

Does the money influence this?

Not so much. The trust is designed to encourage its participants to be net contributors rather than net consumers. It provides very little financial aid, with disbursements generally tied to efforts that enhance one or more family values, particularly: family relationships, learning and growth, or integration of faith and life. This is because I don't see money as a good transmitter of legacy. Character and values are the legacy. Money is a vehicle, not the occupants; a tool, not the substance.

I see the family story as an ongoing demonstration of God's providence in the lives of imperfect people. We've made good choices and bad choices, and both are instructive for developing good judgment. Perhaps more than anything else, our failures highlight God's ability to use all things for his ultimate good purpose.

Recording this kind of story is important to me because I believe my life matters. We've all seen the illustration of the ripple effect of our lives – the concentric circles emanating from a stone thrown into a pond. But there's a stronger illustration for capturing the ongoing value of our legacy. It's the flow of a river, water passing from one point or generation to and through another. The water continually undergoes some degree of change while maintaining its basic identity. As points in the river, we receive and we give. We make our unique contribution; we don't just receive and dam up the flow.

What do you think the impact would be if all families approached their planning as recommended at the Center for Family Conversations?

We would see families loving each other and living out their faith in such a way that the next generation does the same thing. This should cause other high-net-worth individuals to ask, "What do you have that we don't have?" This makes Christ meaningful to up-and-outers. It reproduces abundant hearts that are grateful for the blessings God has given and eager to share them with others.

About the Authors

Tom Conway leads Conway and Associates in assisting families to get clarity around what they believe God wants them to do with their resources.

A CPA by training, Tom has held numerous ministry and financial service positions with such organizations as Ernst & Young, Campus Crusade for Christ, Ronald Blue and Company, Perimeter Church, Generous Giving Inc., National Christian Foundation, Kingdom Advisors, and the Haggai Institute in Atlanta.

Tom has a passion for legacy planning that encompasses five areas: personal, family, financial, business, and philanthropic. As he helps people quantify their needs for the future, what they wish to leave for their family, and how the remainder of their resources can be released to organizations that reflect their values, it often leads to zero-estate-and-IRD-tax situations.

Living and serving in Africa for a number of years and ministering extensively in Europe, Asia, and Russia enhanced Tom's Christian global perspective.

Tom and his wife, Susan, have been married for thirty-five years, have four children and four grandchildren, and live in Atlanta, Georgia.

Steve Gardner is an author, editor, executive coach (CPC), and songwriter. He leads Ambassador Press, the research and communication arm of Ambassador Enterprises. Prior to Ambassador, Steve wrote and edited books, multimedia products, and global training materials for Crown Financial Ministries. He hosted "Three Men and a Book," a monthly radio program and co-hosted "Marriage Matters" with his wife, Maria.

Steve began writing curricula in 1996 as a Vice President with Emerging Young Leaders, and has co-written or edited twenty books as well as dozens of study curricula for books and movies. Steve graduated from Wheaton College with a major in Anthropology.

Steve and Maria have traveled five continents as concert and recording artists, recording 16 albums and performing more than 4,000 concerts and 1,000 TV appearances. They have been married forty-six years and have one daughter and three grandchildren.

Steve enjoys a variety of sports including tennis, racquetball, scuba, and downhill skiing.

Bill High is the Chief Executive Officer of National Christian Foundation Heartland. He works with families, individual givers, and financial advisors to help facilitate God's call to generosity. Much of that work includes advising on issues of legacy planning, income tax planning, business sale planning, and estate planning.

Bill is a visionary leader energized by people and ideas. He loves to learn, innovate, and strategize on how new ideas or new approaches to current methods might escalate growth. As a former lawyer, the law taught him how to ask great questions to find the truth.

As a result of his work with high-net-worth families, Bill founded Generous Life, a legacy-consulting organization. Through Generous Life (www.generouslife.com), Bill consults with families on how to work toward a multi-generational legacy. Bill is also the founder of iDonate.com, a fundraising software company serving the nonprofit community. iDonate.com provides an online marketing solution for nonprofits to market and receive gifts of all kinds, including cash, text, credit card, and non-cash gifts.

A published author and conference speaker, Bill recently authored *Stories of the Generous Life* and is currently working on the follow-up to that book. He is the general editor of *Grants and More for Christian Ministries* and a contributing author to *Three Dimensional Discipleship and Why the Conservative Mind Matters*.

Bill has been married to his wife, Brooke, for 25 years. They have four children: Ashley, Jessica, Nathan and Joseph.

Jerry Nuerge is founder and owner of the Financial Independence Group. He is also the creator of the Wealth Integration and Transfer System™, the Generation Connection Process™, as well as the Revenue Retrieval System™. Jerry holds a BBA and MBA degree, holds the Chartered Advisor in Philanthropy (CAP), is a Chartered Life Underwriter (CLU), a Chartered Financial Consultant (ChFC), a Certified Family  Wealth Counselor (CFWC), and a Registered Investment Advisor (RIA). He is a lifetime member of the Million Dollar Round Table (MDRT), and has qualified for its "Top of the Table." He also belongs to the National Estate Planning Council, the Society of Financial Service Professionals, the National Association of Insurance and Financial Advisors (NAIFA), and is a past-president of the local chapters of these organizations.

Jerry is a member of Kingdom Advisors (KA) and a charter member of the International Association of Advisors in Philanthropy (AiP), which he served as president in 2009.

Jerry has been married to his wife, Sharon, since 1967, has 3 children, and 8 grandchildren, all living in the Fort Wayne, IN area.

Co-author of *Family Wealth Counseling: Getting to the Heart of the Matter* and author of *The Priceless Gift*, Jerry is active as a consultant and national speaker.

Ryan Zeeb is CEO of Camelot Portfolios and Munn Wealth Management.

Ryan has spent the last ten years assisting entrepreneurs, family businesses, professional athletes, beneficiaries, and executives with issues related to financial and investment management, wealth transfer, and risk management.

Ryan is a sought-after speaker and executive coach on the topics of Heritage Planning, Building Professional Collaborative Teams, Professional Practice Development, and Business Real-Growth Strategies.

Prior to joining Camelot, Ryan was President of The Heritage Institute, which he helped to position as the premiere leader in the wealth-consulting and wealth-transfer industry. As President, Ryan led the creation of the Certified Wealth Consultant professional designation. Having trained and consulted with over 400 wealth professionals from around the world, he has built strategic relationships with some of the top institutions in banking, asset management, estate planning, financial planning, executive coaching, nonprofit, and marriage and family counseling.

Ryan most enjoys working in a team environment to coach families, athletes, and professionals to exceed their desired outcomes. He graduated with a B.A. in Business Administration and Finance from Taylor University, where he played baseball and later served as an assistant baseball coach. Ryan enjoys spending time with his wife and three children in outdoor activities and active involvement in church.

Praise for unHeritage

Our company consults with private family business owners of significant net worth. The ideas presented in unHeritage will be tremendously helpful to our client families (and to any family looking to make wise long-term decisions). I plan on encouraging all of our clients to read it.

Thanks to the authors for their time and leadership in this area.

Scott Hamilton
CEO, InKnowVision, LLC

These authors write with great experience and wisdom. Because relational challenges can undermine even the best tax and financial planning, it is critically important that anyone leaving a legacy think deeply about the questions that unHeritage asks and answers.

Tim Voorhees, JD, MBA, AEP®
President, Voorhees Family Office Services, Inc.

Leaving a legacy is not an option; everyone leaves a legacy. The authors have done a masterful job of identifying 11 pitfalls to avoid, enabling us to leave a legacy consistent with our core values. One benefit of dealing with these pitfalls earlier rather than later is the opportunity to live our legacy of choice today – experiencing joy and fulfillment daily. I will share this book with many families from coast to coast.

Alan Pratt
President, Pratt Legacy Advisors

Praise for unHeritage

This book is a must read for families that desire to leave a true legacy and heritage for future generations. Reading this book and navigating these eleven pitfalls should be done BEFORE you implement a comprehensive estate and wealth transfer plan. Doing so will dramatically improve the likelihood that such planning will ultimately be a blessing, and not a curse, to the family and others.

Michael King
Attorney, The National Christian Foundation

Having worked in the arena of generational planning for 35 years, I can wholeheartedly attest to the concepts shared in this book. The soft side, the human side, the relational issues – always trump techniques if one wants to leave a legacy that lasts.

Russ Crosson
President and CEO, Ronald Blue & Co.

unHeritage speaks to the importance of looking beyond the financial statement, which is what traditional estate planning has been about. All advisors (tax, legal, investment, insurance) should rally around families to tackle what's most important: family continuity and the passing of values. This book should be required reading for anyone providing advice for estate or legacy planning or for families seeking more in their estate and legacy plans.

Tim Ash
CEO, Ash Brokerage Corporation